Ontario
Blue-Ribbon
Fly Fishing Guide

Scott E. Smith

"*All streams flow into the sea, yet the sea is never full.
To the place the streams come from,
there they return again.*"

—*Ecclesiastes 1:7*

Ontario
Blue-Ribbon
Fly Fishing Guide

Scott E. Smith

Frank
Amato
PORTLAND

Dedication

To Antonietta:
for her continual encouragement; endless patience, and unselfish support.

Acknowledgments

The author extends much gratitude to all the individuals, organizations and companies that have assisted me in making the completion of this project possible.

To my wife Antonietta, for encouraging me to write, expand my horizons and to take on this project.

To Nicolette, Erin and Timothy, for sharing in their Dad's love for fly fishing and the outdoors.

To Bob Linsenman, a fellow writer and fisher, for his deep friendship, mentoring and paternal guidance.

To Bruce Miller, my closest friend, for sharing his knowledge of fishing and secret places, and for many hours on the stream.

To Bill Boote, for getting me interested in fly fishing, and for years of good friendship.

To John Valk, for sharing his vast knowledge of fly fishing in Southern Ontario, for the countless hand-drawn maps, flies, instructions and telephone calls, I am greatly appreciative of his help.

To Barney Jones, a kindred spirit, for his friendship and guiding efforts; to Larry Halyk, a true gentleman, for his notes and dissertations on Southern Ontario steelhead waters, and his friendship; to Bob McKenzie, for his hospitality and guidance on the river, and for lining me up with so many reputable people; to Terry Kluke, a high-school friend, for many days of guiding on Wabigoon Lake for elusive giant musky; to Roy De Giusti, for guiding me on the Credit, and for his flies and Southern Ontario hatch chart; to Bill Regoza and the Northern Ontario Native Tourist Association, and the late Emmanual Jacob for the Winisk River trip; to Dr. Paul Morgan, for the great trip and hospitality at Blue Fox Camp; to Cam Hawkins and the Journeys End Corporation, for accommodations on several occasions while researching this book; to Gayle and Pat Waters, at the Little Inn of Bayfield, for comfy accommodations and wonderful food; to Judy and Rob Bastedo at Crimson Maples, for lovely accommodations and spectacular breakfasts; to Doug Garlick and Kathleen McFadden at the Red Rock Inn, for all their help; to Ned Basher at the Rossport Inn, for accomodations; to Pat Hron at Cedar Point Lodge, for guiding me on Eagle Lake for musky and pike; to Ted Knott, for guiding me on the Bronte and the Credit; to Geoff Bernardo and Ed Snucins for their knowledge of aurora trout; to Eric Di Carlo, Dave Gonder, George Ozburn and Jon George, for their knowledge of steelhead streams; to Bruce Hole and North of Superior Tourism, for their assistance; to Karl Vogel, a superb guide and angler, for his vast knowledge of the St. Mary's and surrounding rivers; to Rick Novak, for his friendship, and photographic skills; to Fred Dean, for the Northern Ontario hatch chart, and his advice on entomology; to Kurt Melancon for his Nipigon brook trout sizing chart; to Rob Swainson for his knowledge of Nipigon River brook trout; to Eric Eppert, for his knowledge of trout streams in the Sault Ste. Marie area; to Ian Martin, for his knowledge of entomology; to Mike Sewards, for teaching me how to fly fish for steelhead, and his friendly tutorage on the river; to Chris Marshall, for his knowledge of garpike fishing; to Rick Kustich, for his knowledge of the Niagara River; to Romeo Rancourt, for his flies; and to all the members of the Thunder Bay Fly Fishing Club for being such a good literary audience over the years.

To mom and dad, for all their encouragement, and for buying me my first fishing rod.

And lastly, and most importantly, to God, from whom all my blessings, talents and inspiration ultimately come.

About the Author

Scott Smith is a freelance writer who lives in Thunder Bay, Ontario with his wife Antonietta and their three children. His articles have appeared in several fly-fishing and outdoor publications, including, *Fly Fishing, Fly Fisher, American Angler, Wild Steelhead and Salmon, Midwest Fly Fishing, Warm Water Fly Fishing, Ontario Out of Doors,* and *Canoe and Kayak* magazine. Scott is a regional correspondent for *Wild Steelhead and Salmon,* and a field editor for *Midwest Flyfishing.*

He is a member of Joan Whitlock's *Speakers Bureau,* and is active on the fly-fishing lecture circuit.

Needless to say, Scott is an avid fly angler and spends a great deal of time fly fishing his home waters along the north shore of Lake Superior. He runs Superior Fly Fishing, a guide service that specializes in fly fishing opportunities in this area. In a recent book by Bob Linsenman and Steve Nevala, *Great Lakes Steelhead: A Guided Tour For Fly Anglers,* Scott was featured as one of the top guides in the Great Lakes region.

Scott is a veteran police officer with Thunder Bay Police.

Published in 1999 by:
Frank Amato Publications, Inc.
PO Box 82112 • Portland, Oregon 97282 • (503) 653-8108

Cover photos: Scott E. Smith
Fly Plates: Jim Schollmeyer
All other photographs taken by the author unless otherwise noted.
Book Design: Kathy Johnson

Softbound ISBN: 1-57188-162-X Softbound UPC: 0-66066-00360-7

1 3 5 7 9 10 8 6 4 2

Table of Contents

Hudson Bay

43

POLAR BEAR PROV. PARK

42

Lake Nipigon

44

48 52
47
QUETICO PROV. PARK   3 5 6 7 9
Thunder   4 8   10
Bay ⊙ 1 2   11   PUKASKWA PROV. PARK
45   LAKE SUPERIOR PROV. PARK
46   49
                                    12
                                    13
                        14 15 51
Lake Superior   16 Sault Ste. Marie   ⊙ **North Bay**
                     17 18 ⊙ 50   53
                                                   ALGONQUIN PROV. PARK

                        19

Lake Michigan

                                    Lake Huron
                            23   22 20
                            24 60 21
                                61   35
                                         34
                        56 57 58
                        25   ⊙ **Toronto** ★ 33
                        26 54   32
                            Hamilton ⊙   41
                        27 55 31 **Niagara Falls** ⊙
                            59 30 29
                               28
                                    Lake Erie

Section One: Coastal Treasures

Lake Superior Streams

1. McIntyre River
2. McKenzie River
3. Wolf River
4. Black Sturgeon River
5. Lower Nipigon River
6. Jackfish River
7. Jackpine River
8. Cypress River
9. Gravel River
10. Steel River
11. Prairie River
12. Michipicoten River
13. Old Woman River
14. Pancake River
15. Batchawana River
16. Chippewa River
17. Goulais River

Lake Huron & Georgian Bay Streams

18. St Mary's River
19. Manitoulin Island Streams
20. Nottawasaga River
21. Beaver River
22. Bighead River
23. Sauble River
24. Saugeen River
25. Nine Mile River
26. Maitland River
27. Bayfield River

Lake Erie Streams

28. Big Creek
29. Grand River
30. Whitemans Creek
31. Nith River

Lake Ontario Streams

32. Bronte Creek
33. Credit River
34. Rogue River
35. Duffins Creek
36. Oshawa Creek
37. Bowmanville Creek
38. Wilmot Creek
39. Ganaraska River
40. Shelter Valley Creek
41. Niagara River

Hudson Bay and James Bay Streams

42. Winisk River
43. Sutton River

Section Three: Inland Frontiers

Northwestern Musky and Pike

44. Wabigoon Lake and Eagle Lake

Quetico Bass

45. Quetico Provincial Park Waterways

North of Superior

46. Arrow River
47. Shillabeer Creek
48. Frazer River
49. Pukaskwa River
50. East Goulais River
51. Upper Chippewa River

Nipigon's Giant Brook Trout

52. Upper Nipigon River

The Blue Lake System

53. Blue Lake System

The Blue Ribbon Grand

54. Upper Grand River
55. Middle and Lower Grand River

Southern Ontario Trout Streams

56. Upper Credit River
57. The Forks of the Upper Credit River
58. Other Areas on the Upper Credit River
59. Whitemans Creek
60. Upper Saugeen River
61. Beaver River
62. Cold Creek

Ottawa

62
40
9
Lake
Ontario

Map

Bob McKenzie releases a nice steelhead on the Ganaraska River, a prolific steelhead nursery stream
just a short drive east of Metropolitan Toronto.

Introduction

Ontario, one of Canada's ten provinces, stretches from longitude 82 and latitude 42 at its extreme southeastern tip near Leamington Ontario at Point Pelee National Park—the most southerly point in Canada—to longitude 88 and latitude 56 at its extreme northwestern corner; spanning a total of 1,068,580 square kilometers. Within the confines of this vast tract of land one finds a multitude of extremes in weather, geography and wildlife, including fish. To be exact 158 species of fish. From large coastal brook trout rivers sweeping through the tundra of the far north towards Hudson Bay; to farm meadow brooks stocked with brown trout gurgling under highway bridges along the Queen Elizabeth Way near metropolitan Toronto—it is all one place: Ontario. From garpike to largemouth bass; from arctic char and grayling to muskellunge and northern Pike, steelhead, salmon (both Atlantic and Pacific), brook trout, brown trout and a whole lot more; they are all here to be pursued with a fly rod.

Ten million people live in Ontario—a full third of Canada's population. But to be specific, the greatest majority of these people live in the southern belt of the province within fifty miles of the U.S. border. In the remaining tracts of sparsely populated wilderness, countless streams, rivers, lakes, ponds and creeks are found. The average population density in Ontario is 9.4 persons per square kilometer. This means that in many remote areas of the province the population of black bears likely exceeds that of humans. And black bears do little fishing.

Ontario's fishing resources were first tapped into by British Royalty around the turn of the last century. Its lakes and rivers were touted by the Canadian Pacific Railway and the Canadian National Railway for their trophy fish and unspoiled wilderness to wealthy European tourists. Since then millions of people, both resident and non, have enjoyed Ontario's fishing. The world-record brook trout was caught in Ontario waters; world-record muskellunge—yet to be caught—roam in some of her lakes;

and world-class fishing for smallmouth bass, northern pike, steelhead, brook trout and brown trout can be readily obtained by the fly angler. One just needs a little direction on where to begin.

The primary purpose of *Ontario Blue-Ribbon Fly Fishing Guide* is to serve as a guide for the fly angler. Few, if any, guide books have been written about an area that is so vast and diverse. Subsequently the book is not a systematic run-down of every fishable piece of water in the province: This would be a prodigious task resulting in a book thousands of pages long, and too expensive for the average angler to purchase. Rather, *Ontario Blue-Ribbon Fly Fishing Guide* is meant to serve as a guide to the premier fly-fishing opportunities in the province. As fly angling is no longer focused on trout and salmon angling, as it once was, the book will also cover some of the more popular warmwater species that have proven worthy opponents on a fly rod. Nonetheless, coverage of salmonid fly fishing has been apportioned aptly to reflect their popularity with most fly anglers.

In identifying which areas to cover in this book, the following criterion was applied to ascertain whether or not the opportunity was worthy of mention: Accessibility; proximity to/and availability of guide services, fly shops and outfitters; esthetic acceptability; and ability to withstand considerable fishing pressure—either by the existence of special regulations, remoteness, aggressive stocking programs, or the sheer abundance of fish. I also felt that species of fly-rod-amicable game fish that were unique or unusual to Ontario deserved mention; for example the aurora trout and the garpike. Without sounding too apologetic, it is impossible to give due credit to all fly-fishing opportunities in the province in one publication; rather, the primary objective here is to provide a guide to the highlights, and to serve as a base on which to expand.

To put the size of the Province of Ontario into perspective, visualize the states of Texas, Minnesota and Michigan combined and placed on top of Ontario: they would just fit. The countries of England, France and New Zealand would also work for this equation.

To add to the size dilemma, Ontario is inundated with lakes and rivers. Looking from a satellite, one would notice Ontario is ribboned with rivers, streams and creeks along the shores of the Great Lakes and along the Hudson Bay and James Bay coast. The northern part of the province is jewelled with legions of blue diamond-like lakes embedded in Canadian Shield. Consider Michigan: truly a fly-fishing paradise, blessed with many beautiful trout streams flowing into the Great Lakes Basin. Ontario is seven times that of Michigan in area.

I can vaguely recall as a young boy, my dad's '52 Pontiac sitting at the back of our home in Winnipeg, Manitoba. The Manitoba license plate on the back of this round, green automobile, bore the catch phrase "Land of 100,000 Lakes." This was in direct retort to Minnesota's license plate that at the same time boasted "Land of 10,000 Lakes." It was rumored that Ontario put an end to this friendly competition by threatening to manufacture license plates that read "Land of 250,000 Lakes."

All things considered: Ontario is a fly-angler's paradise. No matter where you are in the province, you can rest assured that there is some respectable fly fishing to be had nearby. Even if you are in downtown Toronto, with a metropolitan population of nearly three million people, the fly-fishing aficionado can find solicitude knowing that somewhere nearby are some rising trout or migrating steelhead. In direct contrast, those anglers that have answered the call of the North and travelled to perhaps the shores of Lake Superior or the catchment streams of Hudson Bay, are really in no-man's land. This cornucopia of opportunity and variety of species, no matter where you travel, is where Ontario's wealth in fly-fishing experiences exist. There is so much to explore and so much to learn about that it boggles one's mind. You may choose to stay in a comfortable inn or hotel in a quaint Northern Ontario town and spend your days trekking streams and lakes teaming with wild brook trout. You may be in Toronto on business or perhaps catching a Leafs or Blue Jays game, and still within an afternoon—or an hour depending on the season—be into some dynamite fly-fishing action. After filling your boots (or waders)

with streamside pleasures, you can then return to the city for a gourmet meal, and *The Phantom of the Opera* at Pantages Theatre. If you are the be-one-with-nature type, you can go the way of the true pioneer: Carrying all your provisions on your back or in a canoe, and really experience the wilderness of Ontario. If you choose this route take warning: Come prepared. There are no fly shops in Quetico Park in case you run out of tippet material. There are no phones or electricity in much of Ontario's far north. Forgetting to pack your fly reel or breaking a rod takes on a whole new meaning when you are floating down the Winisk River two-hundred miles from Hudson Bay, sixty miles from the nearest phone and three-hundred miles from the nearest fly shop.

In many ways fly fishing has been slow to arrive in Ontario. Fly fishers being somewhat of an anomaly; I attracted strange looks and comments from other anglers when I first began plying the waters near my home town of Thunder Bay with a fly rod. Fly fishing is an old sport, but in some circles a forgotten one. But as the popularity of fly fishing spreads across North America, more and more people are digging their ancient fly gear out of the attic or dropping a few dollars at the nearest fly shop. For these folks and those that are "old-hats" at the sport, Ontario lies in waiting—like a new frontier—for those who will cast her waters.

Being an undiscovered frontier has obvious advantages, but there are more subtle advantages as well. Within all frontiers, pioneers are compelled to make new trails, develop new techniques and discover new fish for which to cast. Without the inherent trappings of following old tradition, Ontario's fly anglers have developed some intuitive augmentations to the sport that are certainly worthy of mention in this book.

Presently Ontario's wealth lies in its raw materials: Lumber, minerals, and hydroelectric power; and in the south of the province, in its factories. But its future wealth lies in tourism. And as more of the world becomes densely populated with each passing decade, its travellers, modern day explorers, will look for solitude in wilderness: Places like Ontario.

It is important that both the river-keepers and the rods of Ontario work in unison to preserve and enhance its wealth in wild things.

Prince Arthur and his entourage on the Nipigon River, 1918.

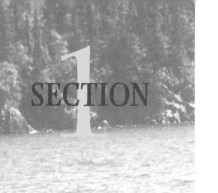

SECTION 1

Coastal Treasures

The bright, clean colours of a Nipigon River brook trout.
Opposite page: Tim Smith with a 24-inch Labour Day coaster brook trout.

Considering that approximately three-quarters of Ontario's immense border is either the coast of Hudson Bay and James Bay, or the shoreline of four of the Great Lakes, a great deal of the available fly fishing in the province is within the catchment tributaries of these bodies of water. Numerous species of game fish and bait fish inhabit these waters. The significant species for the fly angler are of course the salmonids, both resident and migratory.

Within the tributaries of Hudson Bay and James Bay—part of the Arctic Ocean—the premier species for the fly angler is the brook trout. Actually a char (*Salvelinus fontinalis*), the brook trout in these rivers and streams are generally large and generally easy to take on a fly. In many of the long and large tributaries, such as the Winisk River, it is difficult to know whether or not the brook trout are resident or migratory (from Hudson Bay). It is generally felt that most spawning voyages of oceanic brook trout are not lengthy. Subsequently, if you are only miles from the salt, you may be indeed fishing over migratory brook trout.

"Brookies," the nickname for brook trout, does not seem to suit these specimens that often attain weights of five to eight pounds. A brook trout of this size demands respect and is a sight to behold,

especially when adorned in fall colours. Few fish are as precious as the brook trout.

The brook trout in these tributary streams are totally wild. No stocking programs, no genetic tinkering: pure, wild fish.

Almost the entire southern border of Ontario is defined by the shores of four of the Great Lakes: Lake Superior, Lake Huron, Lake Erie and Lake Ontario. In contrast to the Hudson Bay and James Bay fishery, most of the salmonids pursued by anglers—except for wild brook trout and lake trout—were introduced around the turn of the last century. Steelhead, which thrive in all of the lakes, are the most sought-after species by the fly fisher. Although stocking programs still enhance the populations of steelhead in the lower Great Lakes, they have adapted to their respective regions and have become self-sustaining. On the Ontario shore of Lake Superior no stocking of steelhead has been done since the turn of the century. Subsequently, these fish are now considered wild and fight appropriately.

The fly angler that frequents Ontario's Great Lakes tributaries will encounter numerous species of salmonids, including: Steelhead (migratory rainbow trout), Atlantic salmon, lake trout, brown trout, brook trout, and three species of Pacific salmon: Coho, Chinook and pink. In addition, many of these streams host resident populations of rainbow, brook and brown trout, as well as a number of warmwater species.

Having said all that, the successful fly angler must still know which tributaries host which species of fish—and when. This is where the advantages of networking and the keeping of an accurate fishing log come into play. The fly angler must also know the techniques, flies and lies, in order to be successful.

Subsequently, when fishing Ontario's coastal streams it is always wise to hire a guide. In fact, when fishing certain wilderness rivers, to not hire a guide would be remiss, even foolhardy. Many anglers have travelled considerable distances and invested considerable fishing time only to find later that they had been fishing above a barrier to migratory fish, or fishing water that was otherwise barren for a number of varied reasons. These scenarios can be avoided easily with the employment of a reputable guide.

It is always prudent—whether you're guided or not—to ensure that you are fully aware of the fishing regulations applicable to the water you are fishing, and to abide by them.

Techniques

Although the basic principles of fly fishing are in essence applicable to fishing Ontario's coastal streams, one needs to be especially proficient with two basic fly-fishing techniques: Short-line nymphing and the wet-fly swing.

Many of Ontario's Great Lakes tributaries are freestone spate rivers; almost exclusively in the case of the Lake Superior drainage. All migratory fish runs are triggered or influenced to some extent by freshets of runoff; either from heavy rains or snow-melt. Subsequently, much of the fly fishing for migratory salmonids requires skills and techniques appropriate for plying pocket water, plunge pools and other holding water. The most suitable technique is short-line nymphing. Short-line nymphing is a method of presenting a fly on a dead-drift with as little drag as possible at the bottom of the water column where salmonids are located in their holding lies. The basic equipment required for this technique includes: A long (nine- to ten-foot) fly rod, usually in the seven- to nine-weight class; a floating line; and a long leader, anywhere from nine to fifteen feet in length. Dependent on the situation, the use of a foam or cork indicator is also effective. It is not critical that the leader be of the tapered variety— as required for dry-fly fishing—but often the leader is constructed starting with heavy butt material and then stepped down to a suitably strong and abrasion-resistant tippet. Generally split shot is added to the leader to get the system down to the bottom of the water column, although in some situations a weighted nymph will suffice. Attaching split shot to a short dropper line will result in fewer lost flies. A good way to tie in a dropper line is to use a triple surgeon's knot between the leader and the tippet, leaving the tag end of the leader intact. An overhand knot placed at the end of this two-inch dropper will prevent the split shot from sliding off while casting. (See Figures 1 & 2)

The presentation is made by casting upstream of your target holding lie, then by implementing various mending techniques the system is allowed to dead drift with the current, as any nymph or natural egg would. Although the absolute best way to present the fly to a holding fish is to cast from a position slightly upstream and across from the holding lie, presentations can be made from directly across or below the target.

The tuck-cast is an absolute must for this type of fishing. This specialized cast allows the fly line and leader to land upstream of the fly, which enables it to sink drag-free. The tuck cast is implemented by arresting the forward cast just as the loop is beginning to straighten. An abrupt backwards and upwards snap of the wrist is used to accomplish

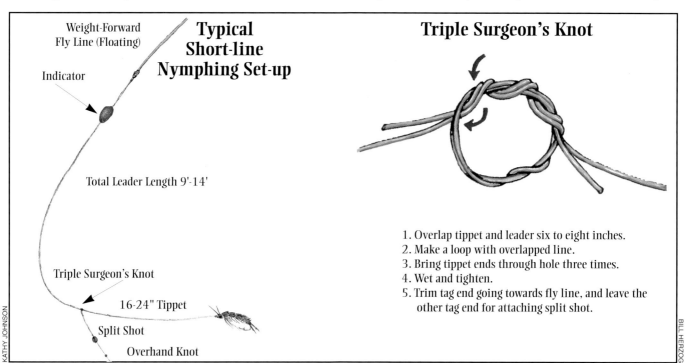

Weight-Forward Fly Line (Floating)

Typical Short-line Nymphing Set-up

Indicator

Total Leader Length 9'-14'

Triple Surgeon's Knot

16-24" Tippet

Split Shot

Overhand Knot

KATHY JOHNSON

Triple Surgeon's Knot

1. Overlap tippet and leader six to eight inches.
2. Make a loop with overlapped line.
3. Bring tippet ends through hole three times.
4. Wet and tighten.
5. Trim tag end going towards fly line, and leave the other tag end for attaching split shot.

BILL HERZOG

Kurt Mclancon swings a streamer through some current seams on the Winisk River.

this. Tuck casts are particularly effective when using an indicator.

A common angler error when fishing the short-line nymph technique is to attempt to fish water too far away—or across current—from the angler's position. In such cases the effect of current (drag) is greatly accentuated, often resulting in the fly scooting far above any holding fish. It is far better to wade closer to the holding lie, than to attempt long casts with this technique.

When short-line nymphing, think of the indicator—or in the absence of, the fly line—as a dry fly that you are attempting to fish drag-free; this will assist you in ensuring the fly is also drifting drag-free. Your indicator or fly line should be drifting slightly slower than the surface water: this is a tell-tale sign that indicates the fly is near the bottom of the water column, which is always slower in current speed.

The wet-fly swing is also very effective in fishing coastal streams; especially in the fall when the fish are more aggressive or when fishing water that holds brook trout, brown trout or resident rainbow trout.

There are several ways to present a fly on a wet-fly swing; however the techniques I will focus on here relate to the use of sinking-tip and shooting-head lines.

Often when trout in deep, large rivers with heavy current are not keyed in on any type of insect hatch, their holding lies are near current seams created by structure, or the confluence of conflicting currents. As the prime holding lies in these situations are generally deep, the angler also needs to present his fly deep. The best method for swimming a large nymph or baitfish imitation in this situation is on a fast-sinking portion of fly line—either a sinking-tip or a sinking shooting head. Full-sinking lines are not recommended for river fishing as they cannot be mended and are difficult to handle in current. Fast-sinking portions of fly line in smaller

lengths (two, four and six feet) can be added to sink-tips and shooting heads to increase their sink rate. These are known as mini-tips. Unless you are fishing extremely clear water for very spooky fish, a short leader, three to six feet long, is necessary to maximize the effect of the sinking fly line. If your leader is too long, the fly is lifted in the current, thereby defeating the purpose of the sinking line, which is of course to get your fly down deep.

Presenting a wet-fly swing with a sink-tip or shooting head is made by making an across-stream cast, immediately mending slack into the line (usually an upstream mend) to allow the fly to sink, and then following the drift of the line (or swing) with your fly rod. Imparting action to the fly with your rod tip will often elicit strikes from hesitant fish.

The depth of the fly can be adjusted by casting farther upstream if you want your presentation deeper, or by casting more downstream if your presentation is too deep. Anglers that are very proficient with this technique can often fish water that may be considered too deep and fast for fly fishing. Experimentation with very fast sinking, shooting-head lines—such as Scientific Anglers' Deep Water Express series—has allowed fly anglers to effectively work stretches of water once thought only fishable with spin-fishing techniques.

Casting sink-tip lines and shooting heads is quite a departure in style from casting a floating line. When casting these heavy lines you must slow your casting stroke down considerably. Use a side arm motion on the back cast, wait for the line to straighten—fully loading your rod—and then use an overhead motion on the forward cast, deliver the line high, to allow for better trajectory and distance. With some practice, casting distances of eighty to ninety feet can be routinely accomplished with shooting heads and sink-tips.

Lake Superior Streams

The author fishes a favourite steelhead run on the Cypress River (Lake Superior).

The rivers and streams of the Ontario north-shore of Lake Superior are what I refer to as my home rivers. They are pristine, wild, rugged and mysterious; their tea-stained pools beckon you to work them with a fly. I am in love with these rivers. To live the perfect life would be to fish every day of the northern season from April to December, plying the many streams on the north-shore; never tiring of the variety of species and places to fish.

The majority of Superior's coastal streams are freestone spate rivers of steep gradient; a product of the terrain through which they traverse being the most rugged portion of the Canadian shield. Giant mesa and questa rock formations tower above Superior, sometimes 1000 feet above the lake. This makes for some spectacular vistas along the Trans-Canada Highway, which skirts the top of Superior, and some very rugged country. The rocky terrain and swift currents of these rivers command respect from all anglers. The spruce bog origins of these tributaries dictate tea-stained, acidic water, reminiscent of Canada's east coast salmon rivers. They are pristine and unpolluted; having a relatively short run between the lake and the first upstream barrier to migratory fish. These tea-stained spate rivers are oligatrophic (non-fertile) in nature: Meaning the acidic water is not fertile enough to support substantial numbers of resident fish; hence reducing the amount of predation on trout and salmon fry. This factor, combined with prevailing gravel bottoms and clean, fast water percolating through the tailouts of pools and runs, completes the requirements for ideal nursery habitat for a cornucopia of salmonids. Brook trout, lake trout and whitefish are native to Lake Superior, but since the turn of the twentieth century, rainbow trout (steelhead), coho, Chinook and pink salmon have been successfully introduced and have evolved into self-sustaining populations. Presently no stocking occurs along Superior's Ontario coast. Some larger rivers, such as the Nipigon and the Steel, attract a small number of Atlantic salmon and brown trout that have been introduced elsewhere on the lake, and because of more fertile conditions host good populations of resident trout.

A study on steelhead in the 1990s—crafted by Ontario Ministry of Natural Resources biologist Jon George—showed that some of the rivers on the shore hosted steelhead that had spawned up to six times. This relates significantly to a very healthy population of wild steelhead. Interesting data also shows that rivers with the most angling pressure, but also the highest rate of catch and release—such as the Cypress and the Jackpine—have the highest incidence of repeat spawners within the population. Jon George, who has become renowned for his steelhead conservation efforts, maintains that the key to keeping the population healthy is to keep it wild. In other jurisdictions on the Great Lakes, domestic strains of rainbow trout have been aggressively stocked to augment the wild population, and offset high harvest. The lugubrious result, in some cases, is a population of impure steelhead inadequate for Superior's rugged conditions, eventually leading to a near collapse in the steelhead population in some areas. The key, of course, in keeping the strain wild is minimal harvest. George's study recommended a very low daily limit on steelhead, while maintaining angling opportunities. This strategy differed greatly from strategies in other jurisdictions where seasons or rivers were closed in an act of frantic crisis management.

Coaster brook trout that once thrived in most of the Great Lakes maintain a foothold in Superior's north-shore tributaries. Significantly in the Lake Nipigon-Nipigon River-Nipigon Bay (Lake Superior) continuum, where it is still possible to catch a brook trout of leviathan standing. "Coasters" is the regional name for the migratory brook trout that thrive along Superior's coast most of the year and ascend coastal rivers in late summer and early fall to spawn. Many coasters attain trophy size—over twenty inches and five pounds—and are eager to smash a passing fly. In past centuries the harvest of these magnificent fish was tremendous, if not ludicrous. As recent as the early 1990s, an angler was allowed to possess five brook trout of any size in one day. This translates (and often did) to five coasters totaling an aggregate weight of twenty-five pounds. Persistent lobbying by angling groups such as the Thunder Bay Fly Fishing Club, resulted in the limit on large brook trout being reduced. However, an earlier closing on the season and a liberal limit (5) on coasters under twelve inches still presents a burr-under-the-saddle for the general populace of fly anglers. Hopefully this management strategy is replaced by policies with stronger conservation and angling opportunity orientations.

There are far too many rivers, streams and creeks along Superior's Ontario coast to mention in this chapter. Almost every one of these tributaries receives a run of one or more species of salmonid; from tiny little creeks fully enveloped in overhanging tag alders, to the mighty Nipigon, the largest tributary of Lake Superior.

Beginning in April, and like everywhere varying from year to year due to prevailing weather conditions, steelhead begin to run north-shore streams. In the beginning they mill around the mouths of their nursery rivers, and slowly filter into the lower pools. The season's length is dependent generally by water volume and temperature. The ideal spring is a slow, gradual melt, interspersed with spring rains, which keeps the rivers fairly high and cool. In low-water years the run can be short-lived, especially if there is a sudden warm spell that brings the water temperatures near the fifty-degree mark. As described to me by one of the most ardent steelheaders on the shore, the peak of the run culminates at the point in time where no more snow exists in the high country. Once this happens the water temperature in the streams increases markedly; nature reminds the steelhead there is little time left before the rivers drop to their summer levels. On some streams, such as the Jackpine, an increase in water levels by ten-fold is not uncommon during the height of spring runoff.

The scenic Steel River flows through some rugged rock canyons in its upper reaches.

Lake Superior Streams

Healthy, wild steelhead spawn up to six times in some rivers on Lake Superior's north shore.

This factor presents a dilemma for the fervent steelheader: to be present at the peak of the run, but not during flood conditions. During the spring of 1996, the north-shore received an incredible runoff due to record snow levels and relentless rain. When most rivers should have been receiving the peak of the steelhead run, they were brown and torrid, sweeping over their banks through the woods and washing out bridges and highways. A scant week later they were fishing perfectly.

Generally the run begins to come into fruition in mid April. Beginning first with the tributaries in the lower latitudes at both ends of the lake near Thunder Bay at the west end, and near Sault Ste. Marie at the east end. As you move north from these points in either direction along the coast you move north in latitude. The run's peak is naturally delayed accordingly as you move north. This provides a fairly lengthy window of opportunity for the angler who begins with the earliest rivers and follows the runs as they move north, even though the run is generally less than one month long in any given stream. In normal years the fishing lasts right into June, with the Steel River being the final river to peak.

After the spawning run is complete, anglers should focus on larger rivers such as the Steel, Nipigon and Michipicoten, which hold a decent number of resident trout and steelhead due to their size and biological profile. River mouths are much overlooked by fly anglers in this region. Lake trout, brook trout, salmon and steelhead are attracted to the mouths of larger rivers and take advantage of the insects and baitfish that are being delivered to them nicely by the river currents, particularly after a good rain. Surf-casting (or flats fishing) is a viable method for working river mouths, but by far float-tubing gives you the most mobility. As Murphy's Law dictates, the fish are always out ten feet farther than you

Coaster brook trout, such as this twenty-incher, still thrive among the shores and tributaries of Nipigon Bay on Lake Superior.

Cam Hawkins fights a fresh coho in a tributary estuary of Lake Superior in late summer.

can cast; this problem is eliminated with the employment of a float tube. Needless to say, you must be wary of windy days on Superior.

Beginning in mid-August—dependent on water levels—coaster brook trout move into their nursery streams, holding in lower pools and estuaries. Although during any period of high water throughout the summer, fishing reasonably sized streams will produce both coasters and steelhead. Pink salmon are the next species to enter streams in late August. Pinks are most prolific during odd years (i.e. 97, 99), but also are found in respectable numbers during even years in larger rivers. Coho salmon, which average about four pounds in Superior streams, are encountered in rivers as early as September 1, peaking somewhere around the end of that month. These fish provide great sport on a fly rod and are generally underutilized by anglers. Lake trout also enter streams during late September. Look for lakers in slow pools in lower sections of rivers. Chinook are found in many of the larger rivers and are becoming more and more popular with fly anglers as special- ized techniques and fly patterns are developed for these beasts. The operative month for Chinook is October in most rivers. Accompanied by any of these runs of fish are steelhead. Fall steelhead on Superior's northern coast are usually smaller than the steelhead found during the spring run, but these chrome dynamos fight like a spring fish of twice their size. I have literally chased after five-pound steelhead as they rocketed their way downstream after feeling the steel, zipping from one holding pool to another trying to escape the stumbling fool who has interrupted their autumn voyage. These battles have left me gasping for breath, but pumped. The embrace of a chrome fall steelhead makes for a glorious "Kodak moment" set against the red and yellow foliage of autumn.

The best steelhead rivers are those that are large enough to provide an over-wintering environment for steelhead. Many rivers receive false runs of two-year-old steelhead that feed on nymphs and salmon eggs, but the larger tributaries receive runs of fish that hold through the winter in deep pools and spawn very early in the spring. A prime example of this type of situation is the Steel River. The best

timing for steelheading on these hold-over rivers is in November, after the salmon and trout have fin- ished spawning. Although a six-pound fall steelhead is considered a large fish during this period, some as large as ten or eleven pounds are reported annually. Freeze-up is usually late November or early December, depending on the size of the river and the onset of winter-like temperatures. The Nipigon River is one of the few rivers that does not freeze over completely during the severity of January's cold spell. Subsequently, winter fishing is only feasible during mid-winter thaws on the Nipigon and a num- ber of select spring creeks in the area.

Fly Patterns

The majority of popular steelhead flies for Superior streams are either egg patterns or bright attractor patterns; although somber-coloured nymphs will also produce fish. Stoneflies are natural to most streams because of their requirement for freestone habitat. Some very large *Pteronarcys dorsata* (giant salmon fly) nymphs up to three inches in length have been collected in several streams along the shore. Golden stoneflies, early brown stoneflies, and March stones are common throughout; subsequently stonefly nymph patterns should be fished in a variety of sizes, as they are well represented in north-shore streams. Numerous caddis and mayfly species are also widespread (see hatch chart in Appendix A), and imitations of the nymphal stage of these insects should also be fished. At one time virtually all flies fished for steelhead in the area were bright egg patterns, the ubiquitous Glow Bug being the standby in every fly box. However, several anglers have transported flies and technology from Michigan streams and have come to the pleasing realization that Superior's steel- head do take nymphs. Due to the prevailing fast water and rocky bottoms of these streams, simply constructed nymph patterns are the most practi- cal ties for these streams. A pattern that I developed to imitate several species of stonefly nymphs—and a quick and easy tie—is the Spring Stone. This is somewhat of an adaptation of the Spring Wiggler, which is also a good fly to fish in these streams. Other patterns such as Mike's Stone, Montana Stone and the Caddis Larvae Nymph also fall into this

The Steel River railway bridge just south of the Trans-Canada Highway.

A colourful, autumn rainbow trout taken on an Egg Sucking Leech from a Lake Superior tributary.

same simple-but-effective category. The logic behind these simple flies is that firstly, intricately tied flies are too easily lost—as are all flies—and take too long to tie at the bench, and secondly that in the fast-flowing waters of spring and fall, steelhead do not have much time to either take or reject the pattern.

Attractor patterns for steelhead are best tied in brighter colours such as fluorescent orange and chartreuse. Even though more and more anglers are warming up to nymph fishing, the egg/attractor category of

A thick-bodied Superior steelhead taken on the author's Cactus Fly.

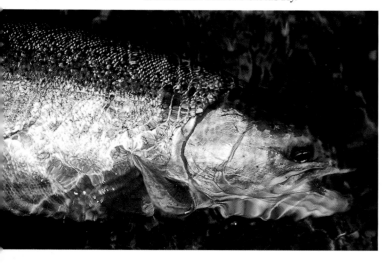

steelhead flies remain the meat-and-potato fly for the steelhead fly angler. One of the most popular patterns is the Cactus Fly, which is simple to tie (consisting of only Cactus Chenille and filoplume or marabou) and very effective. I fish this fly religiously both when prospecting a holding lie or when working visible fish. A number of patterns utilizing the light -reflective and undulating Cactus Chenille (also sold as Ice Chenille) are equally effective. Patterns constructed with this material can be tied full without being too bulky: Bulkiness being undesirable in fishing fast water as it inhibits sink rate. In bright fluorescent colours they are extremely visible in turbid water.

The size of steelhead patterns in Superior's north-shore streams is not as critical as in other Great Lakes fisheries, such as Michigan for example. I have tried my flashy attractor patterns in Michigan streams and watched steelhead scoot under the bank at the sight of these psychedelic flies. Superior steelhead can be taken readily on larger flies (likely due to stained waters), allowing the angler to fish hooks up to size 6 or 4, which will ultimately result in fewer lost fish. As a rule I fish larger, brighter flies in high water or when working a deep holding lie, and conversely fish smaller, more somber patterns, in low water or when working visible fish.

These same flies will produce fish in the fall, however streamers—particularly large rabbit strip or marabou patterns—are very effective, especially when swung through pools and runs on a sink-tip line. Borger's Strip Leeches, Zonkers, Mickey Finns, Muddler Minnows and Egg Sucking Leeches in large sizes are all productive patterns. Most visitors to the shore come poorly equipped with small flies; fish streamers on long-shank hooks anywhere from size 8 to 2 depending again on water clarity and depth. One of my favourite patterns for fall steelhead, trout and salmon is a fly that Bob Linsenman and I developed known as the Green-Butt Monkey. This pattern is as outlandish as its name, but produces particularly well in the prevailing dark, tannic waters of these tributaries. It incorporates all the required elements of a successful fall fly for this area: size, action and colour. A tan-coloured ram's wool head contrasts nicely with the water and gives the fly some bulk. I advocate that a fly that moves water attracts fish, the same principle that makes a spin-fishing plug so effective. I favour the use of rabbit-strip flies over all other patterns in the fall because of the way they come alive in the current, especially when swung or retrieved with some added action imparted by twitching the rod tip.

During the summer months, universal match-the-hatch strategies work fine in these streams.

McIntyre River

As you travel east along the north-shore from the Canada-U.S. border crossing on Highway 61, the first worthwhile tributary is the McIntyre River, situated right in the middle of the city of Thunder Bay. Primarily the McIntyre (known as The Mac by those who know her intimately) is a spring steelhead river. The first fish encountered are right after ice-out in mid-April. Often these are dark over-wintering males wearing a wide band of red on their sides. The run in the McIntyre is the earliest along the west end of the shore and is relatively short-lived. Generally the run peaks at the end of April or the beginning of May, and only fishes well for a couple of weeks. In the years just after the stocking of the Kaministiqua River (a major tributary flowing into Superior at Thunder Bay) with Chinook salmon, the Mac had some exciting salmon fishing during the first week of October, however this has not become an annual occurrence.

The McIntyre is a fun river to fish during the steelhead run. It is small and spirited with lots of open areas for fly fishing. Hooked steelhead of any respectable size make long, exciting runs as the river's pools and runs are relatively shallow and do not provide much refuge.

McKenzie River

The picturesque McKenzie is situated 30 kilometers east of the city of Thunder Bay along the Trans-Canada Highway. If you look directly below the highway bridge you will note that the McKenzie flows a staircase-like path through a rocky canyon as it tumbles down towards Superior. Numerous pockets and pools created in these rock formations provide good spawning and holding water for migratory trout and salmon. The McKenzie gets a good run of steelhead around the end of April/beginning of May; a run of coaster brook trout and pink salmon in late August/early September; a decent run of lake trout, coho salmon and some Chinook later in September and October. It also fishes well right up to freeze-up for fall steelhead. I have also taken some darkly coloured rainbow trout in deep pools in late June. I believe these are resident fish or, if not, at least fish that are taking a summer vacation in this charming river. Some nice brook trout are also present in decent numbers during the summer months.

Wolf River

It seems every fly-fishing mecca has a Wolf River. Our's is a lovely medium-sized, tannic-stained stream that looks a lot like an east coast salmon river. It has beautiful rust-coloured gravel throughout its length with wide sweeping bends cleared of trees on the inside track allowing a nice back cast. The Wolf is typical of streams that flow through gravel eskers in that the high water in spring clears the banks of trees and scours deep bend pools. These pools can exceed six or seven feet in depth and harbour both migratory and resident fish. The steelhead run in the spring is good but often cannot be fished effectively because of high turbid water. When the Wolf is clear and moderate in level it fishes beautifully, especially in the upper reaches of the river north of the highway. The lure of the Wolf is in its fall steelhead and salmon fishery. Beginning in late September and early October, Chinook, coho and steelhead move into the river. It is a river that fishes very well after a fall rain. During the summer some nice trout fishing (streamer and dry-fly action) can be had for respectable

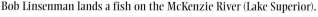

Bob Linsenman lands a fish on the McKenzie River (Lake Superior).

A mint-bright coho salmon fresh from Lake Superior.

rainbows and brook trout right from the lake to the falls, some 8 kilometers upstream from the highway. Sadly a lot of resident fish are harvested each summer particularly those in close proximity to the highway.

Black Sturgeon River

Like the Wolf River, the Black Sturgeon flows into Black Bay on Lake Superior. The steelhead from Black Bay are large for Superior standards, and the Black Sturgeon River is the water to work if you're looking for a trophy steelhead. In the fall the Black Sturgeon is one of the best rivers for large steelhead. Catches will generally not be large in numbers, but the chances of hooking a steelhead in the eight- to ten-pound class are very good, especially in November after the Chinook have completed their spawning run. The Chinook run in October is substantial; some wide, shallow runs and riffles providing some ideal fly-fishing conditions for Chinook. The Chinook and steelhead in the fall are accompanied by a small run of coaster brook trout and pink salmon. When fishing the Black Sturgeon in the fall, I prefer a swimming pattern like a Marabou Spider in Mickey Finn colours, swung systematically through pools and runs on a sink-tip line. This river is one of Superior's larger tributaries, and the wet-fly swing provides a practical method for covering a lot of water.

The author fishes a favourite stretch on the lower Nipigon River.

The steelhead in the Black Sturgeon will move nicely for a seductively swung fly.

The Sturgeon also gets good spring runs of steelhead, but like all the larger tributaries, your timing must coincide with low, clear water. Also similar to the Wolf, when the Sturgeon is running high it is turbid and virtually unfishable. To be frank it can be downright dangerous if you are not careful where you wade.

During late spring and summer the Black Sturgeon fishes well for brook trout and resident rainbow (in the 20-kilometer stretch from the dam to Lake Superior). You will also encounter bass and walleye in the slower stretches of the river.

The upper reaches of the Black Sturgeon system provide some excellent brook trout habitat. There is much to be explored in this system if you can read a map and have a reliable four-wheel-drive. The Shillabeer Creek, detailed in Chapter 8, is a fine example of the excellent resident brook trout fishing in the Black Sturgeon watershed.

Lower Nipigon River

From Alexander's Dam to Nipigon Bay on Lake Superior is a 25-kilometer stretch of the famous Nipigon River, home of the world-record brook

Nipigon River brook trout have a penchant for large streamers.

A salmonfly *(Pteronarcys dorsata)* from the Nipigon River.

trout. The river's clear, wide, powerful waters appear at first to be gentle and forgiving, but once you wade into this magnificent and sometimes formidable river you will soon learn to respect her omnipotence. The average flow at Alexander's is 12000 cfs (cubic feet per second). In years of low flow, the Nipigon fishes like a world-class blue-ribbon river, with gorgeous runs, gravel bars and prolific hatches. Unfortunately the demands for hydroelectric power dictate high water levels that tend to encumber the best hatches. Nevertheless the fish are always present and can be hooked with regularity if you adapt your techniques properly.

During non-hatch periods the best approach is to swing large rabbit-strip patterns through deep current seams and beside structure. The fish in the Nipigon, to a great extent, are bank oriented. Deep holding lies a few feet from the bank provide ideal feeding stations with protection from predation and relentless current: providing nicely all the needs of a trout. Whether you are fishing from the bank or working the shoreline from a boat, cautiously cast quartering downstream and place your fly right beside the shore. Often a trophy-sized rainbow or brook trout will be stationed there.

Chapter Nine will deal more extensively with the brook trout fishery, both present and past, in the Nipigon system. In the lower stretch of the river, the giant brook trout the river has been made famous for, have been replaced to some extent with large resident rainbow trout and summer steelhead. There is some debate as to whether the rainbows are resident or transient Superior fish, but regardless of their citizenship they are ass-kickers on a fly rod. I have taken rainbows in mid-summer on dries and streamers anywhere from five to eight pounds. They immediately go airborne when they feel the hook and rip off backing in seemingly endless runs. These are chunky well-fed fish, a testament to the prolific tailwater conditions provided by the damming of the river. (Not all progress is negative.)

The evening hatch on the lower Nipigon in June and July can be incredible. Clouds of caddis come off the river starting about two hours before dark, which can be as late as 11:00 p.m. in this latitude. Giant Salmon flies are encountered on the water during this same time period, primarily in the evening, but also to a lesser extent during mid-afternoon on cloudy days. These Giant salmonflies (*Pteronarcys dorsata*) are some of the biggest of the species you will encounter anywhere; the adult insect often being a full three inches in length. In fact, a good friend of mine, Mike Sewards, momentarily mistook these insects for some type of "water-bat" the first time he fished the river during this hatch. When the Pteronarcys are coming off the water in good numbers you can rest assured all the biggest trout in the river will be keyed in on them. They provide a very worthwhile meal for a trophy trout, which often will not move to the surface for lesser offerings.

Considering the lack of fly-fishing pressure, surprisingly enough the trout in the lower Nipigon can be very selective. I have spent countless

Lake trout are common catches
on large streamers in the Nipigon River.

Some good dry-fly water on the lower Nipigon River below Alexander's Dam.

evenings trying to figure out what exactly the fish were rising for. As most ardent dry-fly anglers can attest, watching chunky trout boil around your fly time after time can be very frustrating until you find just the right presentation or pattern. I like to fish dries on the Nipigon's clear, flat surface on a downstream presentation with a long leader (up to sixteen feet). Early in the evening you should run a fairly light tippet—say 5X—and your leader should be treated with floatant right up to within two feet of the fly. I leave this portion of tippet without floatant so that it sinks slightly in the surface film and is not so evident to the fish. Quite often I have found that fussy fish are not taking off the surface at all, but are actually taking subsurface emergers; switching to a Floating Mayfly Nymph or a Timberline Emerger under these conditions will often result in hookups. During a good evening or morning hatch on the lower river you will encounter rainbows, brook trout and whitefish. The latter sometimes exceeding five pounds. This interesting combination of species adds to the mystique of the Nipigon.

Steelhead also spawn in the Nipigon and can be encountered year-round in the lower river. Steelhead are taken near spawning lies in April, May and June on egg and nymph patterns, but a more productive time for steelhead on the Nipigon is post-spawn. In early to late June

The Jackpine River: One of the fastest-flowing rivers in Ontario.

(depending on the year), post-spawn steelhead will smash a black Woolly Bugger swung deep on a sink-tip line with reckless abandon. Because of the size of the river and the amount of feed in this tailwater section, the steelhead recover quickly from the rigors of spawning and fight exceptionally well. A ten-pound steelhead in the Nipigon will leave you trembling at the knee, and well into your backing. Biologists feel that the river gets a run of summer steelhead and it definitely gets a run of large aggressive steelhead in the fall. During summer I have encountered bright chrome fish as well as deep-bodied, colourfully detailed rainbows. I can only assume that the latter are resident fish and the sleeker, brighter fish are summer steelhead.

I have seen Chinook salmon in the river as early as July and in fact have spotted dead spawned-out fish on the shore during this period as well, however the bulk of the run does not begin to enter the river until late August. During the start of the run in August and September the Chinook remain in deep holds, but do come to a fly, especially a large flashy smelt pattern. In late September and October Chinook are visible on virtually every piece of spawning gravel. Although they are finicky, they can be taken on flies during this period, either by swinging large streamers in front of their beds or by drifting subtle nymphs or egg

Casting on the lower Nipigon River.

patterns through pods of more skittish fish. Often fresher, more eager takers are situated just downstream from a busy spawning bed. Try prospecting these areas with a large Olive Hare's Ear or Stonefly Nymph, or even an Egg Sucking Leech.

During the same time frame (from August through October), the river also receives a good run of coaster brook trout and lake trout, which enter the river to spawn. Fall steelhead, in turn, enter the river to feed on loose salmon eggs and nymphs kicked adrift by spawning salmon and trout. These steelhead are especially abundant and feisty during the post-salmon-spawn period from late October until December. While fishing the lower Nipigon in the fall, you may encounter any or all of the above species on any given outing. It is important to review the regulations prior to your outing on the Nipigon as there are several fish sanctuaries—to provide safe spawning habitat for brook trout—and varying closing dates for individual species. If you hook an after-season brook trout be sure you land the fish as quickly as possible and release it without any undue handling—or without any handling at all—if possible. Barbless hooks are always a good idea when fishing rivers in late fall where brook trout may be present.

During the winter season (from December to April in these northern latitudes) fishing the Nipigon is possible on mild, unseasonable days. If

Jerry Kustich lands a Jackpine River steelhead while the author's dog, Lightning, looks on.

your thermometer creeps above freezing, the Nipigon will provide a midwinter reprieve for those suffering from the morose effects of fly-fishing withdrawal. I have tobogganed my boat down to the river over waist deep snow on more than one occasion for this therapeutic purpose, and have actually hooked fish as well.

Access to the lower Nipigon is best for the walk-and-wade angler at Alexander's Dam, situated 16 kilometers north of the Trans-Canada Highway on Highway 585, or from accesses near the bridge at the Trans-Canada Highway. Angling from a boat, however, gives you much more water to fish, as many gravel bars and islands midstream are only accessible by watercraft. Due to the lack of take-out points, a non-motorized drift boat is not practical on the Nipigon; large square-stern canoes or small fishing boats equipped with a ten or fifteen horse motor are the most commonly used vessels. Good boat launches are situated both at Alexander's Dam and at the municipal dock in the town of Nipigon.

Jackfish River

Venturing even farther east—and into the no-man's land of the north-shore—the first respectably sized river you'll encounter will be the Jackfish. From the highway it appears as a slow meandering stretch of "frog-water," but by taking a canoe equipped with a small motor upstream several miles you will experience another face of this river. The upper Jackfish is a scenic stretch of classic trout water: beautiful runs and riffles connecting deep pools held in granite formations. This stretch of the river fishes well in late spring after the runoff subsides for steelhead, resident rainbow and brook trout. In late summer, coaster brook trout and coho salmon begin moving upstream with the onset of cooler water temperatures and freshets of rain. The deep pools and runs in the canyon of the upper river provide permanent residency for some large rainbows that are deeply shaded in varying hues of purple with vermilion flanks. The resident rainbows are not as prolific as their smaller brook trout counterparts, but one encounter with one of these striped denizens will make your trip worth the work required to reach this stretch of the river.

Jackpine River

The Jackpine River with its steep gradient and thundering volumes of water during the heights of spring runoff is an impressive sight. As you look north from the Trans-Canada you will see where the river has cascaded down through towering castles of ancient diabase rock, which is unique to the north-shore of Superior. The continuous erosion of these rocks and the existence of natural gravel eskers provides for ideal spawning gravel. The entire length of the Jackpine River from the lake to the first barrier to migratory fish (some 15 kilometers of river), is ideal spawning habitat for steelhead. Consequently the Jackpine has the best run of steelhead along the north-shore.

The annual steelhead extravaganza on the "JP" (as it is affectionately known by her faithfuls) begins—again subject to seasonal variables—

about mid-April. The river gets a run of big hens at ice-out and fishes decently until the peak flow of spring runoff makes the river virtually unfishable. Once the river has peaked and begins to drop however, the fishing is absolutely outstanding. Jackpine steelhead seem to grow legs when hooked, and in the fast continuous pocket water of the JP, anglers are well advised to wear "running shoes" for wading boots. The run continues into mid-May with some decent fishing for drop-backs until the end of the month. Even into June the lower river will receive a rush of fish if a heavy rain swells her banks.

Similar to all rivers that flow into Nipigon Bay, the JP receives a good run of coaster brook trout in late summer. During high water periods throughout the summer, the river fishes well for fresh coasters and smaller steelhead that sneak into the lower river with increasing water levels. The mouth of the JP—which over the years has changed several times due to flood conditions—is especially productive for lakers, steelhead and brookies for most of the fly-fishing season. Large and flashy streamers are best fished behind a float tube on a heavy sink-tip line or shooting head. Steelhead will blow instantly into your backing when hooked in the big water, making this particular type of angling especially addictive.

Late September and throughout October brings good numbers of lake trout, coho, pink salmon, and steelhead into the Jackpine.

Cypress River

Resisting the selfish temptation to avoid mentioning this beautiful river altogether, here I go selling national secrets. The Cypress is a gem for the fly angler. It has a nice gradient, a lovely combination of pools, runs, riffles and pocket water, combined with lovely spawning gravel and peaceful setting. Similar to many other north-shore rivers, it flows through a heavy sand and gravel deposit—remnants of the last ice-age. The sweeping effects of spring runoff, clear many of the banks for nice back casts, and scour deep-pocketed bend pools.

Primarily the Cypress is a nursery stream, therefore it fishes best during spring steelhead runs and autumn runs of coaster brook trout, lake trout, whitefish, coho and pink salmon, and of course fall steelhead. Similar to the Jackpine, the Cypress has one of the best runs of steelhead

Michigan writer Bob Linsenman admires a brisk flow on the Cypress River.

Erin Smith with a late-run Chinook salmon from the Steel River.

Cam Hawkins with a spectacular Cypress River coaster brook trout.

on the shore. Jon George's study on steelhead on the Canadian shore of Lake Superior identified both the Jackpine and the Cypress as having very healthy runs of steelhead. George's study, which evaluated the status of the population by the percentage of repeat spawners, found that both of these rivers had steelhead returning to spawn for up to six times. This is a very significant factor for maintaining a good population that can withstand several poor spawning years back to back. The Cypress steelhead run is slightly later than the Jackpine; generally fishing very well throughout the month of May.

Again typical of all rivers that flow into Nipigon Bay, the Cypress receives a run of coasters anytime summer rains result in a good flow. The Cypress has the best run of coaster brook trout on Lake Superior, except for perhaps the Nipigon. The coasters seem to be thriving even though up until the early 1990s the bag limit was a ridiculous five fish per angler day. Coasters that return to the Cypress from late August to late September average roughly eighteen inches with many fish exceeding twenty-two inches. Coasters are sleeker than Nipigon fish and therefore do not have the same weight-per-length ratio; subsequently a twenty-inch coaster weighs roughly three and one half to four pounds.

This wonderful river also receives a very good run of lake trout, pink salmon and coho salmon in mid to late September. I have had many twenty-fish days on the Cypress when these runs are peaking.

Gravel River

The Gravel River is also a gem to fly fish providing the river is not exceedingly high and dirty. It can blow high and turbid during the peak of runoff or after a torrential rain. Unlike the Cypress and the Jackpine, the Gravel fishes fairly well throughout the low-water periods of summer. It has a larger drainage, and above the first barrier to migratory fish at the power line above the Trans-Canada it fishes well for resident brook trout. In fact you can hike for days along the upper Gravel if you are so inclined. This area of Ontario has no roads to speak of above the Trans-Canada so be sure to stick to the river if you are exploring.

The east branch of the Gravel River flows through a huge canyon some 25 kilometers long north of the Trans-Canada Highway. This region of the Gravel is rarely explored due to its inaccessibility, but for those willing to go to great lengths to float this section of the river, the brook trout fishing is rumoured to be outstanding.

The Gravel receives a run of large steelhead in the spring, fishing well right into late May and early June, and receives runs of coho, brook trout and steelhead in the fall. It holds decent-sized rainbows and brook trout throughout the summer months in its deepest pools.

Steel River

Reminiscent of some of the famous Atlantic salmon rivers on the east coast of Canada, the Steel is a beautiful and large, tea-stained river. Its flows are unfishable during the peak of spring runoff, but after her levels drop—and immediately after ice-out in April before her levels rise—the Steel is a steelheader's wilderness paradise.

The Steel fishes best for steelhead in late May and early June in the upper reaches of the river, at least an hour's walk north of the Trans-Canada. The barrier for migratory fish is a large set of falls at the base of Santoy Lake—a deep, cold, substantially sized body of water. Subsequently, the river temperatures remain relatively cool throughout the summer; a boon to populations of resident rainbow, brook trout and runs of summer steelhead. Spawning steelhead can be found right into late June, long after the runs of steelhead have completely finished in other tributaries. In addition to summer-run steelhead, reports of Atlantic salmon have also been received, including one actual specimen that was brought into the MNR—apparently from the Steel River. It stands to reason that because of the river's size and suitability as spawning water, the Steel attracts fish from all over Lake Superior. Other introduced species such as Kamloops (rainbow) trout and brown trout have also turned up in the Steel.

In autumn the Steel River receives a substantial run of pink salmon, coho and Chinook salmon, as well as a small run of coaster brook trout.

Fall angling on the rugged Steel River.

Although steelhead can be encountered almost any time of the year in this river, the best time for fall steelheading is in November. Like other larger tributaries such as the Nipigon and the Black Sturgeon, the Steel is a good river for trophy fall steelhead in the ten-pound category.

A word of advice to the walk-and-wade angler: the trail along the Steel is steep and rocky, and wading the river can be treacherous most times of the year. One of the favoured pools on the river is aptly named the Hospital Pool, on account of where some of her patrons have found themselves after treating the river with less than due respect.

Prairie River

The Prairie River is a medium-sized stream with conditions conducive to fly fishing providing the water clarity is fairly good. Due to its bank composition, the river can take on the colour of chocolate milk after a heavy rain or during the peak of spring runoff.

The Prairie is noted for good spring steelhead fishing, rainbow and brook trout fishing throughout the summer, and coaster brook trout, lake trout and the three species of Pacific salmon in the fall. Some years the lower stretch of the river can be inundated with lake trout, which will hammer a seductively swung streamer pattern.

Michipicoten River

Up until a few years ago Eric DiCarlo operated a successful guide service on the Michipicoten River for steelhead and resident rainbow trout. Similar to the Steel River, the freestone Michipicoten hosts a run of summer steelhead. Eric developed some interesting techniques and flies specific to the Michipicoten. In recent years Eric has found that the river is not producing as it was a decade ago. We're hopeful this trend will change with the recent lowering of the limit on steelhead and the effects of the

Chinook salmon in the Steel provide great sport for the fly angler during the first week of October when the run peaks. I have found that the Chinook in the Steel take a fly quite readily in comparison with some of the more stubborn fish I have encountered in other Superior streams.

Jerry Kustich fishes the scenic Cypress River Falls.

Coho salmon run many Superior streams in late summer and early fall, including the Michipicoten River.

gin-clear, manageable and wadeable stream. Indeed fly angling on Superior's streams is best done on small to medium-sized streams like the Pancake. During the steelhead run, Karl likes to work the Pancake in late May after the river peaks. Sight fishing is one of Karl's fortes, and the Pancake offers roughly 4 kilometers (2 1/2 miles) of ideal hunting grounds. The river gets a plentiful run of pink salmon in the late September, as well as good numbers of cohos and the odd Chinook. Karl notes that in the fall of 1996, when the St. Mary's River (the outflow of Lake Superior into Lake Huron) was running at almost full capacity, the Pancake received a marked increase in numbers and size of its pink salmon. He suspects that some of these pinks were actually Lake Huron fish that made their way through the locks at St. Mary's Dam.

Batchawana River

The Batchawana is larger than the Chippewa with slightly more colour to the water. It has a larger catchment, and while being somewhat wild and untethered in the spring, offers some decent fly fishing in late spring and early summer. There is approximately 8 kilometers (5 miles) of river to the falls, which pose a barrier to migratory fish. There are few access points, but similar to most of Superior's Canadian shore tributaries the Batchewana is a wilderness river without well-defined trails and backroad accesses. The chance of a brown trout is an additional windfall for the fly fisher.

Chippewa River

The Chippewa has a rather short stretch of water accessible to the fly angler—both north and south of the Trans-Canada—for migratory species, but this stretch fishes well for spring steelhead, fall coho and Chinook salmon, and plentiful pink salmon. The Chippewa also attracts fall steelhead. As compared to the optimum conditions offered by the Pancake, the Chippewa is bigger, slightly tea-stained and turbid during high water. Its attractions, however, include the occasional brook trout mixed in with the regular fare of steelhead and salmon. The Chippewa River is the sight of a parking lot and plaque signifying the center point in Canada of the Trans-Canada Highway.

The stretch above the falls on the Chippewa offers some easily wadeable fishing for resident rainbow and brook trout. Eric Eppert, guide and owner of Fish Tales Custom Tackle, knows this area well and spends a substantial amount of time during the summer, fishing and exploring the scenic upper reaches of the Chippewa. Although fish tend to be small—up to 14 inches—the experience is scenic and wild, with good hatches of stoneflies, caddis and mayflies.

flood in the spring of 1996, which may have rejuvenated its spawning areas with fresh, fine gravel. (Another friend of mine, Dave Gonder, reported some outstanding fall fishing in autumn of 1997 on the Mich. This may be an indication of improved fishing on this river.)

The Michipicoten is truly a fine fly-fishing river, almost as if it was specifically designed as such with the delightful riffle-run-pool configuration so typical of Superior's best streams. The river receives a good run of Chinook salmon, cohos, pinks and lake trout in the fall, and like most larger tributaries of Superior, it receives a decent run of autumn steelhead in October and November. Again similar to the Nipigon and the Steel, the Michipicoten attracts a small run of brown trout. Walleye and smallmouth bass are also represented on a smaller scale.

One of Eric's notable techniques for fishing summer steelhead is to work nymphs on a sinking or sink-tip line. Steelhead rising for emerging caddis on the Michipicoten is a common occurrence, and to the neophyte a difficult hatch to fish successfully. Eric positions himself upstream from a pod of rising steelhead and fishes a caddis nymph emerger pattern on a tight line directly downstream. The effect of current on the sinking line pulls the caddis imitation to the surface in a manner that evidently looks realistic to the steelhead; many hookups are realized with this technique.

Old Woman River

The sight of this fine lady as you drive across the Old Woman River Bridge on the Trans-Canada Highway is enough to make even the most reserved fly angler crook their neck and drive off the road in distraction. It is a medium gradient, gin-clear, classic fly-fishing stream. It fishes well for fresh steelhead prior to runoff, but during the height of freshet in early May it is tough to fish properly. After the runoff subsides however, Eric DiCarlo likes to work nymphs and egg patterns for hungry drop-back steelhead. Years of fishing this river have given Eric the sense that the majority of the steelhead run moves through the river during the height of spring runoff; nature's remedy for reaching high-country spawning grounds. During summer and fall, the river is quite low and does not offer productive fishing except in lower pools after a good rain. It is a shallow river with lots of riffles for spawning fish, but few deep pools for summer residency.

Pancake River

As you continue the scenic tour of the Canadian shore of Lake Superior down towards Sault Ste. Marie, the next fly angling gem is the Pancake River. This is guide Karl Vogel's favourite Superior stream. To the fly angler it offers steelhead in the spring, coho and pink salmon in fall, in a

This male pink salmon in typical spawning form was taken on an olive Gold Ribbed Hare's Ear.

George Ozburn watches Bruce Miller work a good steelhead on the Cypress River.

Goulais River

The Goulais is a big sweeping river for Superior standards. It is as diverse in character as in species. One can fish for walleye, pike, bass and even musky in the slower, more fertile section of the lower river; swing deeply fished flies over steelhead and salmon on midsection gravel bars; or work a dry fly to rising trout on the upper reaches of the watershed.

Canoe tripping is a good way to experience the Goulais, according to Karl Vogel; however a lack of take-out points dictates making the trek an overnighter. Good fishing can be had for steelhead and resident brook trout in the 80-kilometer, middle stretch of the river, between the Trans-Canada Highway and the Searchmont area. Because of the river's size, many of the steelhead enter the river in the fall and over-winter in deeper haunts. The Achigan River, a remote tributary, offers good fall fly fishing for steelhead and salmon.

Whittman Dam, north of Searchmont, is the end of the line for migratory fish. In the section above the dam (the east branch of the Goulais), good numbers of brown trout have been introduced through stocking programs in the early 1990s. The East Goulais is one of a few fly-fishing-only rivers in Ontario. It features easily wadeable gravel runs, riffles and pocket water sections for brook trout, rainbow and brown trout, in a pleasant setting of scenic stands of white pine. Eric Eppert finds the blue-winged olive to be the most predominant hatch on the East Goulais.

Recommended Services

(Refer to Appendix B, page 95, for addresses and phone numbers)

The Red Rock Inn

Conveniently located in Red Rock, Ontario, the Red Rock Inn provides a warm, friendly and affordable place for fly anglers working the streams of Nipigon Bay and points east to dry their waders, catch up on sleep in a cozy bed, and rejuvenate their weary bones with a warm shower and a hot meal. Particularly worthy of note is their chicken entrees, which are plentiful, wonderfully moist and well-presented. The Inn offers accommodations from a basic room tastefully decorated with hardwood floors and classic furniture, to the deluxe rooms with their own gas fireplace, wooden deck and Jacuzzi tub.

The Inn welcomes all outdoor aficionados and offers package prices not only to fly anglers but also to kayakers, hiking groups, rock- and ice-climbing expeditions.

River's Edge Fly Shop

My good friend and fishing companion Bill Boote operates River's Edge Fly Shop, which is conveniently located inside D&R Sporting Goods in Thunder Bay, Ontario. Bill's shop has a substantial stock of rods, reels, waders and, of course, fly-tying materials. River's Edge is an authorized Sage outlet and has a Scientific Anglers Mastery dealership. River's Edge also provides guide service on a limited basis.

Superior Fly Fishing

Since 1995 I have operated a guide service that specifically targets the rivers along the Canadian shore for steelhead, salmon and brook trout. I also guide on some of the interior rivers and lakes for trout and small-mouth. Package trips available through select fly shops in Canada and the U.S. have grown to be very much in demand; in fact I can't keep up, which speaks to the high-quality experience available in this new fly-fishing frontier. I have several top-notch guides that assist me with individual clients and group bookings.

Daily guided trips include instruction, a limited number of flies, and a hearty, delicious meal and snacks. Group packages include accommodations, all meals, and flights from major centers.

Eric DiCarlo

Eric provides guide service on a limited basis on some of the lakes and streams surrounding his home in Wawa, near the banks of the Michipicoten. Eric has specialized in fly fishing for steelhead, and also for trophy pike, which are abundant and cooperative. Eric was featured in *Great Lakes Steelhead: A Guided Tour for Fly-Anglers* by Bob Linsenman and Steve Nevala, as one of the top sixteen steelhead guides in the Great Lakes Basin. Eric is a committed conservationist and is outspoken on his views in regard to the over-harvest of migratory species in his bailiwick.

Karl Vogel

Karl is also a featured guide in *Great Lakes Steelhead*, and in my mind is one of the best steelhead guides and anglers that I have ever met. In fact, I have never encountered anyone as adept at spotting steelhead as Karl Vogel. In addition to his angling skills, Karl is a friendly, amicable person, who offers advice and guidance freely to other fly anglers, whether they are his clients or just someone flogging the same waters as he. Karl is also quite outspoken on fish conservation views, and in all respects is a true ambassador to the sport of fly fishing in Ontario. Karl guides primarily on the St. Mary's River (featured in the Lake Huron chapter), but also guides for steelhead and salmon on some of the productive rivers on the east end of Superior such as the Pancake, Batchewana and Chippewa rivers.

Fish Tales Custom Tackle

Eric Eppert operates a small fly shop out of his home in Sault Ste. Marie, Ontario and carries most fly-tying needs for fishing the eastern tributaries of the Canadian shore. He also provides limited guide service on some of the wilderness streams and lakes in the Sault area.

CHAPTER 2

Lake Huron and Georgian Bay Streams

Karl Vogel on his beloved St. Mary's Rapids.

I n my estimation Lake Huron tributaries offer the most diversity in terrain and stream character. This is due to the change in geography as one travels from the streams of the Precambrian shield near Sault Ste. Marie, south to the rich agricultural countryside streams of Southwestern Ontario. In direct contrast to Superior's rather short nursery rivers, steelhead and salmon from Lake Huron and Georgian Bay can often migrate fifty to one-hundred kilometers to access spawning beds in tributary headwaters. This greatly increases the time in which these fish are available to the fly angler, and provides a large multi-seasonal window for a variety of angling opportunities.

Lake Huron was the first of the Great Lakes to be stocked with rainbow trout; primarily stock from the McCloud River system in California. According to "Rainbow Trout in the Great Lakes," a paper by Hugh R. MacCrimmon and Barra Lowe Gots for the Ontario Ministry of Natural Resources (1972), the first watershed in the Great Lakes basin to receive rainbow trout was Michigan's Au Sable River in 1876. In 1896 rainbows were introduced in several other Michigan (Lake Huron) tributaries, and the first captures of rainbow trout were recorded in Lake Huron and the Au Sable River. In that same decade the first plantings of rainbow trout in Ontario took place in the Nottawasaga River. Coincidental or not, it seems significant that both the Au Sable and the Nottawasaga presently support strong populations of self-sustaining rainbow trout, which we have come to know and love as steelhead.

During the first three decades of the twentieth century, stockings of rainbow trout in Lake Huron continued in various locations within the province. Combined with the natural movement of the species, these stockings established what we now enjoy as a prolific wild run of steelhead in most of Lake Huron's Ontario tributaries. Steelhead that average between six and eight pounds—with numerous fish over ten pounds and the odd fish approaching the twenty-pound mark—are available to the fly angler during both spring and fall runs in many important spawning tributaries. At present the bulk of the Lake Huron steelhead that run Ontario streams are wild, particularly in Georgian Bay tributaries; however some stocking by the OMNR and local fishing clubs occurs in Lake Huron streams, such as the Saugeen, Maitland, Bayfield and Nine Mile rivers. Summer-run steelhead in Huron tributaries are uncommon, with only a marginal number of stray Skamania-strain fish (from previous plantings by the State of Michigan and by private clubs in Ontario) entering some streams in the last week of July and the first week of August.

Additionally, runs of Pacific salmon (Chinook, pink and coho), brown trout, lake trout, whitefish, and in some cases, Atlantic salmon, provide a variety of spirited salmonids for pursuit by the fly angler. With the exception of the indigenous lake trout and lake whitefish, these species were also successfully introduced since the turn of the last century. Chinook salmon, which are still extensively stocked by local clubs primarily for the benefit of open-lake boat anglers, average around fifteen pounds and are present in almost all important tributaries mentioned in this chapter. Coho salmon, which are no longer stocked, have a small self-sustaining stronghold in streams such as the Nottawasaga, Sauble, Maitland and Nine Mile rivers. Pink salmon are present in many tributaries, but not terribly common or popular, except in the St. Mary's, which receives a large and regular run during odd years and decent runs in even years. (Other rivers receive marginal runs in odd years and almost no pinks in even years.)

To add to this cornucopia of fish, many of Huron's more fertile cold-water tributaries, such as the Saugeen, the Beaver and the Nottawasaga, support resident populations of brook trout, rainbow trout and brown trout—offering almost year-round opportunities for trout and salmon buffs. Smallmouth bass, northern pike, perch and walleye (and a number of lesser-known warmwater species) are also eager to smash a fly in many of the warmer tributaries, such as the Maitland and the Bayfield rivers, which also support runs of salmonids during the spring and fall.

Consistent with other regions in the Great Lakes Basin, the steelhead attracts the most attention from fly anglers on Ontario's Huron streams. Lake Huron steelhead are regarded as large streamlined fish that fight hard and fast, and take flies well. In contrast to Superior's steelhead, which seem to have a predisposition for egg/attractor patterns, Huron steelhead are duped regularly with more traditional nymph imitations that represent important insects in each particular river. The reason for this penchant for nymphs comes from the predominant limestone, agriculturally based soils through which many of Huron's tributaries flow. These water conditions make for rich habitat for invertebrates, which in turn provide a forage base for juvenile steelhead and resident trout. According to Larry Halyk, Ontario Ministry of Natural Resources biologist and fly-fishing guru, all of the major mayfly, caddis and stonefly taxa are well represented in the important Huron tributaries. Even died-in-the-wool roe fishermen opt for small black stonefly imitations fished under their floats in early spring.

I first learned about the Huron steelheads' preference for nymphs while fishing the St. Mary's Rapids in Sault Ste. Marie, Ontario. I instantly became addicted to the notion of fishing for salmon-sized steelhead with stream-trout techniques and flies. Beginners to this game still have a hard time accepting the fact that a fifteen-pound steelhead can be hooked—and even landed—on a size twelve nymph and six-pound

tippet. Of course this is not a simple task. After reading this book you will be better equipped with the required knowledge for accomplishing such an angling feat.

Lake Huron and Georgian Bay's important steelhead and salmon runs begin in the north with the St. Mary's River, and include a few tributaries of the North Channel, such as the Root, Garden and Echo rivers. For some reason, steelhead are not prolific in most other streams along the North Channel and southward through the regions of the Precambrian shield. This is likely due to the predominance of walleye, northern pike and other dominant predatory species within the tributaries of this region. Additionally, these bedrock flows lack the existence of good spawning gravel for salmonids.

However, in virtually every agricultural watershed along the south shore of Georgian Bay, around the Bruce Peninsula, and southward along the east shore of Lake Huron to the Ausable River at Grand Bend, Ontario, steelhead populations thrive.

In addition, some streams on Manitoulin Island also have significant spawning runs of steelhead. The best Lake Huron/Georgian Bay tributaries, such as the Saugeen and the Nottawasaga, owe their substantial runs of steelhead to the abundance of natural ground water, which maintains base-flows and cool temperatures for steelhead juveniles. The annual steelhead run begins in September in the hotbed streams of Lake Huron/Georgian Bay, and continues throughout fall, winter and spring—right up until late May during a late spring. Consider October/November and April/May as the operative months for prime steelhead fishing.

Because of the span in latitude between Lake Huron's most northern and southern streams, the timing of steelhead and salmon runs cannot be generalized more specifically, as in the case of Lake Superior or Ontario tributaries. But similarly, the travelling angler can follow the steelhead runs from the earliest fish in the Nottawasaga and the Saugeen in March, to the latest in the St. Mary's at the end of May and beginning of June, and enjoy a long stint of steelhead fishing in both spring and fall. The only limiting factors in these seasonal endeavours will be your pocket book, your employer, and in some cases your spouse. (All of which must be factored into your timing plans unless you are willing to deal with the consequences.) Also unlike Superior streams, which are blessed with a virtual open season for steelhead and salmon in most streams (excepting December 25), open season regulations vary from stream to stream in Huron's drainage. Subsequently I will address the timing issues in each specific stream section in this chapter.

Lastly, accessing the coastal streams on Lake Huron in Ontario, is not as easy as say the streams of Lake Superior, where each stream crosses the Trans-Canada Highway and can be accessed easily at these points. In order to find your way properly through the maze of country roads in rural Southern Ontario you must have a good regional, current road map. In addition, you will need to correspond this map with a current copy of Ontario's fishing regulations to ensure you are fishing in the proper areas of each stream. These regulations are constantly changing, and the season closures, etc. mentioned in this chapter are accurate only at the time of this writing. Additionally, you must always respect private property and ask permission to fish or cross any private land.

Fly Patterns

Generically speaking, caddis larvae imitations are a good bet almost any time on Huron streams for steelhead and salmon. If there is one fly that you should carry in volumes, and in various shades and sizes, it is the Olive Caddis Larvae Nymph. A simple but very effective pattern is created with just two basic ingredients: dubbed olive hare's mask fur for the body, and a peacock hurl thorax. The best hook for the job is a curved, heavy, scud hook, such as the TMC 2457 or the Daiichi 1150; these are sharp and very strong hooks—necessary ingredients for any steelhead and salmon fly. Tie this simple pattern in sizes 14 through 8 in various shades of olive and green, and even bright chartreuse. Substituting ostrich hurl or hare's mask dubbing tied loosely for the thorax material will give you greater variety. If you simply cannot tie such a basic pattern without being

Cam Hawkins honours an airborne steelhead on The Flats, Saugeen River, while guide John Valk offers advice.

overly technical (those of you who are sometimes referred to as techno-weenies by your friends), rib the abdomen with gold wire, or even net some samples from your favourite stream to copy if you desire. I have found some surprisingly bright-coloured caddis larvae under rocks, and yes, even in the bellies of trout (old habits die hard).

The Gold Ribbed Hare's Ear Nymph, and the multitude of variations of same, are also very important to this fishery. A good adaptation of this fly as tied by Michigan writer Bob Linsenman, is a Hare's Ear Nymph tied with olive hare's mask dubbing for the abdomen and thorax, and gray filoplume for the tail. Bob claims that the filoplume tail undulates nicely to represent the swimming motions of many mayfly nymphs. *Hexagenia* nymphs are also important in many of the streams with dams, reservoirs and other areas with silty bottoms.

Stoneflies are always a good pattern for steelhead in freestone sections of streams, and are particularly effective in early spring when the first steelhead enter Huron's tributaries. Tie general stonefly imitations in a variety of sizes and shades of brown and black.

It is important to remember that the nymphs of all species of aquatic insects live in the stream for several years (in the case of some stoneflies up to three years), and hence they are present in a variety of sizes in the stream. To express this in simpler terms, this means that just because you are fishing a stream in April where a giant salmonfly hatch occurs in June, doesn't mean that you should be fishing a three-inch-long nymph, even though the adult is that size when it hatches. The predominant size of salmonfly nymphs in that stream at that particular time may be a one-inch-long specimen. Subsequently you need to carry your favourite nymph patterns in a variety of sizes.

Although dry-fly fishing for steelhead and salmon in Ontario is a new venture, there is a small subculture of anglers that are actively pursuing this endeavour. Steelhead anglers in many streams, particularly in warmer periods of both the spring and fall runs, are taking fish on both dead-drifted traditional dries and waking or Bomber patterns. There is room here for many pioneers and adventurous souls. What you need to know is that Huron steelhead will take a dry fly, so keep some dries in your box during the run.

Streamers are also useful in these moderate periods during late spring and early fall. Spawned-out steelhead in the spring are particularly ravenous in the large tributaries where the return to the lake may involve traversing fifty or more kilometers of stream. Fall steelhead and salmon are also interested in streamer patterns; particularly fall steelhead, which are feeding heavily on salmon eggs and salmon carrion. Other species that spawn in the fall will also smash a bright or gaudy streamer out of aggression, especially male brown trout, Chinook and coho salmon. Good streamers for Huron streams include the Woolly Bugger, Muddler Minnow, Marabou Matuka, Zonker, Strip Leech and a number of West Coast steelhead patterns, such as the Skykomish Sunrise, the Polar Shrimp and the Fall Favorite.

St. Mary's River

The St. Mary's River flows from Lake Superior into Lake Huron; subsequently its water temperatures are cooler than other regional tributaries. The flow on the river is controlled by bottom-draw compensating gates at the top of St. Mary's Rapids, which are used to regulate the level of Lake Superior. Superior's cool, clean, clear water makes for ideal spawning habitat in the rocky, gravel-bottomed stretch of pocket water at the outflow of Superior, known as St. Mary's Rapids. The Rapids is where ninety percent of all the fly angling for salmonids occurs in this large river. This is the pocket-water angler's paradise. There is an abundance of fish available at almost any given time of the year, weather permitting. The most written about is the spring steelhead run. Even Ernest Hemingway wrote about the prolific runs of rainbow trout in the Rapids. To add to the tremendous runs of steelhead in the St. Mary's Rapids, Atlantic salmon, brown trout, resident rainbow trout, whitefish, pink salmon, coho salmon, Chinook salmon and even a rare Chinook-pink hybrid salmon known locally as the pinook, inhabit the rapids at one time or another. This gives the fly angler that has access to the St. Mary's

John Valk with a colourful Saugeen River buck taken on a Caddis Larvae Nymph.

Rapids something to fish for from May until December. I have said more than once that I am actually glad I don't live any closer than seven hours away from the Rapids, because if I did, my work and family would suffer much neglect.

The St. Mary's Rapids start just below the International Bridge between Sault Ste. Marie, Ontario and the Michigan city of the same name. They continue for approximately 1 kilometer (approximately 3/4 mile), and the river averages about 1/2 kilometer in width. Happily (for me anyway) the best fishing occurs on the Canadian side of the river. This is where a concrete burm wall has been constructed to moderate water levels and to ensure sufficient water for proper spawning habitat. The burm wall runs parallel with the flows from near the bridge for almost 750 meters (2500 feet). Fly fishing for all species occurs on both sides of the burm wall; although this will vary depending on the species and the prevailing water levels in the river.

The spring steelhead run in the Rapids begins in late April and peaks towards the end of May. Depending on the year and the water temperatures in Lake Superior, steelhead can be encountered in the Rapids well into June. But for all intents and purposes consider the last week of May and the first week in June prime time for steelhead.

Naturally the steelhead in the Rapids are Lake Huron fish, which typically average about eight pounds but can be encountered up to fifteen, with some approaching twenty. For several years the City of Sault Ste. Marie operated a hatchery on the St. Mary's and stocked some 50,000 steelhead annually into the river. This practice was discontinued in 1996; however wild returns are still substantial.

Conquering the Rapids requires some special considerations. As I mentioned earlier this is prime pocket-water habitat. When water conditions are optimum a good wader can pick his or her way almost halfway across the river fishing prime holding lies throughout. The Rapids are inundated with boulders from the size of a bowling ball to a Volkswagen. Virtually the entire bottom is covered with marble to golf ball-sized gravel. With Superior's cool water percolating throughout, the Rapids is premier spawning habitat. Prime lies are often only waist deep, but even so spotting steelhead and salmon in this clear water is surprisingly difficult. The constant dance of surface reflections can be hypnotic, so the angler must concentrate below the surface and look for movement and shadows. Rather than looking for an entire fish, one is best advised to look for flashes and movement, and perhaps a portion of a fish. With some practice, fly anglers can become very adept at both locating fish and learning their most common lies in the St. Mary's Rapids. Generally these lies are in current seams adjacent to rock outcroppings; in pockets behind boulders, and on gravel flats with broken surface water. Usually the steelhead are quite close to shore (and the burm wall) at first light; subsequently great care needs to be taken so that you don't spook the fish into deeper water prematurely. This will happen eventually anyway as the sun climbs higher and angler activity increases. I have seen several anglers waltz across the burm wall wearing bright-coloured clothing and watched steelhead scamper all over the place as a result. This type of complication can be avoided by wearing drab clothing (leave the fluorescent ball hats at home) and keeping a low profile when moving about on the burm. I have found that the built-in knee-pads that some manufacturers—such as Bare—incorporate on their neoprene waders are an option worth paying extra for.

Once the steelhead have moved away from the edge of the burm and the shoreline, anglers can easily pick up fish by prospecting deep slots and pockets in midstream, and from places like the Canadian Pool where many bright fish stage before moving into the upper section of the Rapids.

Having mentioned that the fish are near the burm at first light, I should add that it is not necessary for everyone to be on the river before the birds. In my experience there seems to be an exodus of morning anglers from the Rapids at about 11:00 a.m., so sometimes it pays to sleep in, go for breakfast, and then attend to some fishing after. Successfully fishing the Rapids is more contingent on your ability to spot fish and make effective presentations to them, than it is to be the first one on the water.

Some people have a preference for prospecting deep water for steelhead, but I must admit that I am hooked on hunting for resting steelhead and salmon, and then casting for them. I learned most of my sight-fishing skills from a good friend and astute student of the St. Mary's—Mike Sewards. Mike is currently a teacher in Thunder Bay, but he grew up in the Sault and spent a tremendous amount of his time on the Rapids. The first time I ever fished the Rapids was with Mike in late May of 1994. I had several hook-ups that day, and many more in the days that followed, but had it not been for his guidance, I'm sure I would have been skunked. The ability to spot fish, cast and mend accurately, and move stealthily about on the immense stretch of clear water is directly proportionate to your success. For these reasons I highly recommend hiring a reputable guide. Safety on this stretch of water is also imperative, and a guide will have the day-to-day knowledge of water conditions and safe passages from one section to another.

In addition to the employment of a guide, a high-quality pair of polarized glasses is an absolute must, as is a pair of studded, felt-soled wading boots. Over and above the rocky-gravelly conditions to navigate, there are some slippery areas with bedrock bottoms, particularly just upstream of the deep Canadian Pool. As for waders, neoprenes are dress code; the temperature on the Rapids rarely exceeds fifty degrees during the spring and fall. A wading staff is also a handy investment. Some people choose to purchase the telescopic or sectional types, but I prefer the shaft of a good hockey stick—something to do with my Canadian heritage I suppose.

Back to the spring steelhead run: By far the most predominant technique for fishing steelhead on the Rapids is short-line nymphing. I

**The Egg Sucking Leech can be a
productive pattern on the St. Mary's Rapids.**

like a seven- or eight-weight rod in the nine-and-one-half to ten-foot category. The longer rods give you better mending capabilities and the ability to lift your fly line off the water to prevent steelhead from wrapping your line around the many rocks in the Rapids. For these same reasons many anglers are turning to Spey rods, as long as your arms can take handling them all day. A weight-forward floating line and a nine- to twelve-foot leader tapering to a six-pound tippet is standard line gear. Normally an indicator is an asset, but at times the relentless winds off Superior make indicator fishing impossible.

Presentations are best made from a position perpendicular to the fish, or even better, slightly upstream of the fish. The proper amount of added weight (split-shot) to your tippet will get the fly down to the fish without hanging up on bottom excessively. If this occurs lighten up on the split-shot and add a slack-line mend to your drift.

Although egg/attractor patterns will take fish, many anglers fish more traditional trout patterns with greater success. According to some fly anglers, egg/attractor patterns worked better on the Rapids before angling pressure increased to its present level. Biologically speaking there is an abundance of caddis in the Rapids, specifically *Rhyacophila*, or green rock worms, and other species, and this makes caddis larvae imitations a wise and productive choice.

Similar to many other Huron streams, steelhead can be taken on dries and streamers during both the spring and fall run.

After the spring steelhead run subsides somewhere around the middle of June the next fish up to bat is the Atlantic salmon. These were first introduced to the river in the early 1990s and since about 1995 anglers have been catching Atlantics on flies with acceptable regularity, at least in Atlantic salmon angler's terms. These fish range between two and fifteen pounds, and are not unlike their East Coast cousins with respect to bravado. They are generally found in deeper sections of the rapids than steelhead, in pools, deep slots and pockets. They are taken with regularity on wet flies and Bomber dry flies, and also on dead-drifted nymphs. Rod considerations are similar to the steelhead anglers', generally in the seven- to nine-weight class.

Karl Vogel, one of the best guides on the St. Mary's (likely one of the best guides you'll find anywhere), has developed a technique for nymphing Atlantics in the deep water below the Sault Edison power house from a small boat. Karl, who has an incredible eye for spotting fish, ties his boat off downstream of the wall and casts to visible Atlantics in holding patterns in the current. He presents small nymphs on light tippets to the skittish fish, and once an Atlantic is hooked, he casts off the moorings and drifts downstream with the fish, that is likely decided to head back to Lake Huron by now. During the summer of 1998 Karl boated 24 Atlantics using this method, and had particularly good success during the Hex hatch. It seems that *Hexagenia* spinners (not nymphs, but spent adults) were being drawn down to the bottom of the river below the turbines and the compensating gates, and strangely enough the Atlantics were taking Hex spinner patterns fished like a nymph near the bottom.

The Atlantic salmon fishing is best on the Rapids between mid-June and the end of July. During this period, resident rainbow trout are also encountered in these same pools and slots. Early August is generally poor due to higher water temperatures in the river.

The end of August brings thousands of pink salmon into the rapids. These pint-sized salmon are often overlooked by many fly anglers, but in the vast numbers in which they are found in the Rapids they are a barrel of laughs. This is an excellent time to bring a new fly angler to the Rapids and get them into fish. Pinks are not tough to hook (although they can be fussy at times), and their average size of three to six pounds makes them great sport on a six-weight rod. Pinks spawn in the Rapids in greater numbers during odd years, but there is still enough of them in even years (2000, 2002 etc.) to make fishing for them a worthwhile venture; especially considering there are fewer anglers in those years. Pinks are found in the same types of holding water as spring steelhead, but often in shallower locations as well. They are normally in pods of between ten and thirty fish, and are taken with the same dead-drift nymph techniques as steelhead. Both egg/attractor and nymph patterns will take pinks. You can often hook numerous fish by continually changing flies once one pattern stops producing. At times a flashy coloured streamer swung in front of the pod will elicit savage strikes from aggressive male fish.

The best time for pink salmon on the Rapids is during the first three weeks of September. Like all Pacific salmon, pinks die after spawning and deteriorate throughout the spawning process until this finally occurs. Subsequently, the best sport is when the fish are fresh in from the lake.

Chinook salmon filter into the Rapids during the pink salmon run in mid-September and often give anglers intent on pint-sized pinks a reel-buzzing surprise. The Chinook reach their peak in mid-October, and the Rapids are choked with them when this occurs. These bad-boys are anywhere between ten and twenty pounds so leave your trout gear at home. Although many seasoned fly anglers still opt for their favourite eight-weight, a stout nine or ten is more in order. Chinook are fished in almost identical manner to pinks and steelhead with the addition of a slight swing or lift of the fly at the downstream end of the drift, particularly in front of holding salmon. This often is the added touch necessary to entice Chinook into grabbing your fly. Chinook can be fussy, subsequently a foul-hooked fish (fish hooked in places other than in the mouth) can be a fairly common occurrence. If this happens, quickly break off your fly or suffer the consequences of breaking a rod (or a leg) chasing a crazed Chinook all over the place.

Large olive Hare's Ear Nymphs, Egg Sucking Leeches, black stonefly nymphs (size 4 and 6) and small egg patterns (such as Karl's Crystal Egg) are the most productive Chinook patterns. Karl Vogel recommends eight-pound Maxima tippet for these brutes.

Coho salmon also migrate into the St. Mary's Rapids during the period between early September and mid-October; however these fish congregate in deep-water holds below the compensating gates at the top of the rapids, and are not easily accessed by fly anglers. Nevertheless they are still encountered in other deep sections of the Rapids, and are suckers for a sweetly swung streamer, either brightly coloured or very dark.

Similarly, steelhead also enter the Rapids in October and November, but generally hold in the same deep water lies as the coho, and offer only incidental catches for fly anglers.

Manitoulin Island Streams

Manitoulin Island is an almost forgotten little corner of Ontario. The streams on this very large island are rarely fished except by island residents and anglers from the City of Sudbury. There are a number of small, tight-banked streams—such as Blue Jay Creek, Shrigley Creek and Silver Creek—that receive good runs of steelhead but the streams that offer more fly-fishing-friendly conditions are the Mindemoya and the Manitou. These two rivers are moderately sized Lake Huron tributaries that under prime water conditions fish just as well as any other good steelhead stream in the province.

The Manitou River, which flows from spring-fed Manitou Lake on the south side of the island, offers approximately 35 kilometers of water to fish during both spring and fall. The river averages between 35 and 45 feet in width and runs almost crystal clear except after a heavy rain, which colours the water slightly. There is a nice mix of water conditions on the Manitou that make it attractive for both fly and gear anglers. Fly anglers are best advised to target the various pocket water and riffle sections of the river. One such section is located in the upper reaches of the river directly below Lake Manitou, and another below White Lake, which is really a

widening of the river a short hike downstream of Lake Manitou.

Additional pocket water sections are located downstream of Government Road. Between these sections are some juicy-looking pools and some bedrock-bottomed sections of river that conversely don't hold many fish. A nice plunge pool with some good pocket water below it is situated roughly one kilometer upstream of Lake Huron. This area fishes particularly well in the fall.

A good early-spring opportunity exists at the river mouth where staging steelhead are often duped by a swung streamer or a dead-drifted nymph.

Dave Gonder, an ardent fly angler that fishes many of the best streams on the island, favours the Manitou, particularly during the fall for bright steelhead. Dave says that the runs on the island, like virtually everywhere else, are dependent on high water levels, so target the Manitou after a healthy fall rain. Manitou River steelhead have a peculiar habit of holding in relatively shallow water. They are often spotted in pockets, runs and inside bends in the gin-clear water. Fall steelhead fishing is generally best in late November and December, with smaller fish entering the river first. Later in the year steelhead up to twelve or thirteen pounds are not uncommon in the Manitou. Quite a Christmas present, I think.

Dave Gonder suggests fishing egg patterns like the Glow Bug in cream, pink and Oregon cheese; stonefly nymphs in size 6 or 8, and general-purpose mayfly nymph imitations. He adds that your particular fly choice is secondary to presentation—which must be near the bottom. Dave uses the short-line nymphing technique with an indicator and a "slinky-rig" (lead shot or pencil lead encased in shrink tubing or parachute cord) to get the fly down to the bottom.

The Mindemoya River, also situated on the south side of the island, conversely, does not have a good fall run and is best flogged in the spring. The river is fed by Mindemoya Lake and has chalky, blue tinge to its water. Subsequently the river is more conducive to prospecting than sight fishing. It also differs from the Manitou by being slightly smaller in width and length, and has a slower gradient. The clay and sandy banks of this river are spiced up by undercut banks, log jams and bend pools that make for some interesting lies for steelhead. Dave likes to fish holding water

The author with a chrome hen near International Bridge

Bill Spicer nymphs the Bighead River in November.

and pockets below known spawning redds, and in some cases has hooked as many as a dozen fish in one pocket. Fly selection for the Mindemoya is identical to the Manitou.

Both the Mindemoya and the Manitou receive healthy numbers of Chinook salmon in September and October.

Check your fishing regulations before fishing the Mindemoya or the Manitou for special closed-season regulations on certain sections of river. Much of the land surrounding both of these streams is private so be sure to obtain permission from landowners before fishing. Manitoulin Islanders have a reputation for being friendly and laid-back, especially towards fly anglers and catch-and-release proponents, so be sure to be cooperative and polite.

A regional topographical map will show many of the back roads that cross these rivers and afford river access.

Manitoulin Island is situated off the north shore of Lake Huron and separates the latter from Georgian Bay. It can be accessed by taking Highway 6 south from the Trans-Canada (Hwy. 17) at the town of Espanola, or you can take the toll ferry from Tobermory if you're coming from Southern Ontario and want to take a break from sitting behind the wheel. (Call 1-800-265-3163 for crossing times and rates.) Accommodations can be found in the towns of Providence Bay and Mindemoya, which are handy to these rivers.

Nottawasaga River

Unlike most other Lake Huron rivers, whose pools, runs and riffles are easily read by most fly anglers, the Nottawasaga is a tough river to read and fish. It has a much lower gradient than other neighbouring Georgian Bay streams, and much of the river has a featureless u-shaped channel, which in many ways explains why it is a favourite with float and gear anglers. However, as my friend Larry Halyk explains, the Nottawasaga has many attributes that make it well worth learning.

The Nottawasaga River, which flows into Nottawasaga Bay near the town of Wasaga Beach on Georgian Bay, boasts one of the largest runs of steelhead in the province. Steelhead enter this river earlier than most others, particularly in the fall when the Nottawasaga receives a large proportion of its run. This early-run trait is due to the length of distance the steelhead must travel to reach their spawning grounds in the head-waters and associated tributaries, such as the Pine, Boyne and Mad rivers. These tributaries, and the upper Nottawasaga itself, are situated in the Niagara Escarpment and are excellent nursery habitat for steelhead. In addition, this river boasts some of the biggest and most powerful steelhead of Lake Huron's stock, which can be very aggressive in the moderate water temperature regimes in September and October.

The Chinook salmon run is also earlier than most other area tributaries and is generally in full swing by late August.

Fly anglers are best advised to concentrate on the lower river near Wasaga Beach Provincial Park, and near the top end of the open-season section of the river near the town of Baxter. Both of these areas offer more easily read riffles and runs. The Nottawasaga has an open—year-round—season from the mouth to the confluence of the Boyne River, some seventy kilometers of river.

This river has a following of astute students from the nearby cities of Toronto and Barrie, so be prepared to encounter some competition during peak times. Fortunately this is a big river and there is room to move and find some measure of solitude. I fished the Nottawasaga in October a few years ago and I found it very much to my liking. I did encounter other anglers, but the olive-tinted water flashed Bright Steelhead like a neon sign and I immediately fell in love.

Beaver River

The Beaver River is another Georgian Bay tributary that is popular with Toronto-area steelhead anglers; particularly the 1/2-kilometer stretch from the Thornbury Mill Dam down to the Bay, which can be shoulder to shoulder when the runs are in full swing. However, the masses fish here for a reason, and that is that this stretch of river is great steelhead water. This medium-sized stream has enough flow and cover to hold steelhead and salmon even when the flows are at a minimum.

The Thornbury Dam, situated in the Town of Thornbury, is of the lock variety. Some steelhead are lifted over the dam giving them access to a considerable amount of river above this barrier. This region of the Beaver is better known for its resident trout fishery (see Chapter 12) so just after trout season opens in April, the upper section of river is a good—and scenic—piece of water to prospect for both steelhead and resident trout. This section is fished quite lightly in comparison with the water below Thornbury Dam.

Bighead River

The Bighead River is truly a Georgian Bay gem. Its steelhead are wild, strong, thick-shouldered fish that never seem to quit fighting. As Larry Halyk so aptly puts it, "to be in the Bighead Valley on a crisp mid-October day forty-eight hours after a good rain, is to die and to go to heaven." He adds, "You will hook fish and many will clean your clock!"

The Bighead flows into Georgian Bay at the town of Meaford. The first 15 kilometers (approximately) of river are open to angling from the last Saturday in April to December 31, which in Southern Ontario is considered an extended open season for steelhead. This section of river falls into the boundaries of St. Vincent County. The first 5 kilometers of this stretch (from the Bay upstream) flow through a beautiful western-looking valley. The river in this stretch is very conducive to high-stick nymphing with an abundance of boulder-studded pocket water. Upstream of St. Vincent Township the river braids into several small nursery streams that provide ideal spawning and rearing conditions for steelhead. This region is also good habitat for resident brookies and brown trout.

Unlike the Beaver, which is slightly bigger, the Bighead is a moderately sized, shallow stream that averages about fifty feet in width. It drains very hilly country, which results in greatly varying flows according to rainfall and snow runoff. For this reason the Bighead is a you-should-have-been-here-yesterday river, particularly during the fall run. Its flows can vary greatly after a good rain, and one should be there on the bank when the river begins to clear and your fly is just visible in a foot of water, as the fish move through the waters of St. Vincent Township quickly in order to access the upstream, protected reaches of the system, where the best spawning conditions are found.

At this writing, a move by the OMNR and some concerned anglers has been tabled to establish a catch-and-release area on the lower Bighead; however the vocal majority of harvest-intent anglers are presenting considerable resistance to this initiative. It is to be hoped that the rate of harvest will be reduced on the Bighead and other Southern Ontario steelhead tributaries so they may reach their full potential. In the case of this fine river, over-harvesting is probably the only factor in the way of making the Bighead an incredible steelhead mecca.

Similar to the Nottawasaga, and other area streams, the Bighead also receives a substantial run of Chinook in September and October.

Sauble River

The Sauble River is accessed off Highway 21 near the town of Sauble Falls and Sauble Falls Provincial Park. It has a low gradient, except for in the vicinity of the falls, and has a reputation for running clear when all other rivers in the area are high and dirty. It is favoured by float anglers and fly fishers because of its sandy bottom and gentle gradient, which is reminiscent of the fabled Michigan streams—the Betsie and the Little Manistee. It has only marginal nursery habitat in its drainage so the runs of steelhead and salmon are not big. However, under the right conditions it fishes quite well.

Saugeen River

The Saugeen River is one of the most popular rivers with steelhead and salmon fly anglers in Southern Ontario, and for good reason. The river is large and scenic, with enough water for steelhead to really perform. Test all backing knots and other terminal gear before fishing the Saugeen, and be prepared to scamper down the bank once a good steelhead grows legs and begins to head for Lake Huron.

The Saugeen enters Lake Huron at the town of Southhampton on Highway 21. From here to Denny's Dam, 4 kilometers upstream, is where 99% of all the migratory fishing pressure takes place on this big river. There are some old bridge abutments a short stretch downstream of Denny's, which mark the upstream limit of a year-round open-season piece of water from there to the mouth, providing a fix for steelhead aficionados throughout the winter. The Abutments also mark a popular spot for steelhead and salmon anglers and a well-maintained campsite is located there, run by the Ontario Steelheaders. Below the Abutments is a small island that marks the upstream limit of the Graveyard Pool, a great place to try your hand at taking a steelhead on a waking Bomber or traditional dry fly. Below the Graveyard Pool is a large riffle, with plenty of pocket water for short-line nymphing when the flows are moderate. Below this riffle is an area known as The Flats, another productive haunt. Downstream from here, on the north side of the river, is Fisherman's Park off Highway 21. This side of the river tends to get a little less pressure, but requires a little more walking to get to the river from Fisherman's Park. Directly adjacent to Fisherman's Park is a stretch of pocket water known as the First Rapids. Downstream of these rapids is another popular spot aptly referred to as the First Island. All of these hot-spots are worth fishing, and the river is easy enough to read for first-timers with its abundance of riffles, current seams, and slots. Like fishing any big river, try and divide the water into digestible segments and fish the water at your feet before wading or making long casts. Often steelhead are right along the bank on this river.

Among other things, the Saugeen is a meeting place for terminal steelhead nuts. Those of us that really get carried away with the pursuit of steelhead in Ontario eventually end up on the banks of the Saugeen. Often it can be quite a social scene, especially late in the fall and during mild days in the winter when only the die-hards are fishing this river. When the steelhead run is in full swing, or worse when the Chinook make their invasion, the crowds are big and less amiable. Nevertheless, this is a big enough place to find room for a backcast even when the word hits the streets that a good run of fresh fish are in.

I've spent some considerable time on this river—both in fall and spring—and have really come to admire it. For its size, the Saugeen does not have a tremendous run of steelhead—perhaps five- to-ten thousand fish—but the attraction is in the freestone nature of this big tributary.

On one particularly productive spring day with John Valk, I hooked several good steelhead (not that there are bad steelhead) in an area known as the Flats above the First Island. Several of these nasty fish made me run downstream for quite a stretch; I even managed to land a few. I also wandered up to the Graveyard Pool, on John's instruction, to slowly work a nymph in the tailout. John gave me a couple of bomber-style dry flies to try, which I stowed away deep in my box as soon as John turned his head. I wasn't about to spend good fishing time playing with surface flies. A few minutes into my nymph fishing, however, a big steelhead flashed underneath my orange strike indicator, and with trembling hands I quickly began re-rigging with an orange bomber. The fish looked like a chrome truck bumper. As fishing stories go (at least my stories) the fish never showed again—but I now fish bombers on the Saugeen with a little more faith.

Above Denny's Dam are literally hundreds of kilometers of fishable river and smaller tributaries that feed this big river. The upper branches of the Saugeen cover this portion of Ontario like a dragnet, right to the Niagara Escarpment. Steelhead fishing above Denny's on the Saugeen is permitted to the Walkerton Dam to December 31, a distance of about 75 kilometers. Thanks to some improvements made to the fishway at Denny's, good numbers of steelhead are accessing this stretch of river which is virtually untapped, although it is prime water. This area is well worth exploring and will pay dividends to those that spend some time doing so. Resident brown trout are also found in this stretch and the many tributaries beyond Walkerton. These areas will be explored further in Chapter 12.

Steelhead are found in the lower Saugeen almost year round, except in the heat of summer, between late June and late August. There are still, however, a few stray Skamanias encountered incidentally at the end of July below Denny's. The first decent numbers of steelhead show up in the lower reaches of the Saugeen by Labour Day. Like most rivers anywhere, the best runs come after a good rain, and these are hard to predict in the fall. Steelhead continue to filter into the river, conditions permitting, throughout the fall and winter, until the freshets of spring bring the biggest runs in late April. The beauty of the Saugeen for the inveterate steelheader is that during low-water periods throughout the main season, the Saugeen has enough water to hold fish. After a heavy rain, however, the Saugeen can flow dark and dangerous making it unfishable for up to a week. Fortunately there are several smaller tributaries in the vicinity, such as the Sauble, that will stay relatively fishable during high-water periods.

Chinook salmon run strong and abundant in the Saugeen in September and October.

Nine Mile River

This small- to medium-sized river has a comparatively impressive steel-head run of anywhere from two- to five-thousand fish. There is a small dam and fishway approximately 1/2 kilometer upstream from the mouth of the river, which is located at the town of Port Albert on Highway 21. A great deal of angling pressure takes place just downstream of the dam, and after a good rain the scene can be comical. Above the dam is a lot of productive water that can be a little trying to fish unless you are used to working streams that are tight with overhanging branches. The Nine Mile is a good alternative river to hit when the Maitland is high and dirty.

Maitland River

The Maitland is a sleeper. If I had been blindfolded the first time I was taken to one of the rugged-looking canyon stretches on the Maitland, I would never have guessed that I was in Southern Ontario. The setting reminded me of pictures of the Umpqua River Valley or some other

John Valk puts the wood to a steelhead on the Saugeen River.

John Valk with a chrome hen steelhead from the Saugeen.

famous western place. The river is made for fly angling, with sweet-looking bends and lots of room for a backcast. In many ways it resembles a big Western river with its rugged canyons and long sweeping runs. It is a river that requires you to pay your dues before it gives up its secrets, or its fish.

There are 50 kilometers of undammed river from its mouth near the city of Goderich on Highway 21 to the town of Wingham. This means that the fish are spread out and not concentrated below dams and fishways like so many other Huron rivers in this region. Big catches are not the rule on the Maitland, but her calling is in the scenery and character of the river. First-timers are well advised to employ a guide, as there is a lot of vacant water between pools and runs. Long walks, unless you are being shuttled in a canoe by a knowledgeable river guide, are the rule when fishing this river. The most ardent students of the Maitland, anglers like Larry Halyk, follow the steelhead and salmon runs as they move upstream. Steelhead have a knack for disappearing in this big river, and this is a mixed blessing: many anglers dabble on the Maitland and soon become frustrated and turn to other, more predictable, haunts.

The lowest ten kilometers of the Maitland, below the town of Benmiller, flows through a deep, wooded valley. The river character in this stretch is wild, with a number of bedrock chutes, deep, dark pools, boulder-strewn pocket water and moderately deep runs. This is a nice place to fish Western style and swing a nymph in a traditional wet-fly manner.

The stretch below Highway 21 is open year round and has a nice cluster of holding pools. This is a good place to start the day and find out from locals if any fresh fish have entered the river. The steelhead season is open from the opening of trout season in April to December 31, from Highway 21 upstream to Wingham.

The steelhead run in the Maitland is approximately 50% wild. This percentage is growing steadily due to some valiant stream restoration efforts by local clubs such as the Maitland Valley Anglers. The Chinook run in the Maitland is excellent, and the shallow, clear character of the water and the wide open spaces make it an ideal theater for this arduous game. Like the Saugeen, this is a big river, making a hooked steelhead or Chinook salmon a sight to behold—with lots of room for them to put on a show. Also similar to the Saugeen, this is a great place to dry-fly fish for steelhead. Both fresh-run and dropback fish in this river will take a dry. Larry Halyk has hooked some double-digit steelhead in early May on small Elk Hair Caddis dries, as the fish tend to hold in pools awaiting a good rain to flush them back to Lake Huron after the spawn. The relatively shallow nature of this river means that the steelhead run is contingent on rainfall for both runs of fresh fish and the descent of drop-backs. During normal flow the Maitland is quite clear, but like all the rivers in this agriculturally based region of Ontario, it runs high and dirty after heavy rains. Smaller tributaries like the Bayfield are good alternatives when this condition prevails.

Typical of the experience most newcomers have had when fishing the Maitland, I did not hook any steelhead on the first few occasions that I fished her. The true pleasure of being on this river is in the fishing, not the catching.

Bayfield River

A short distance south of the Maitland is the Bayfield River, a small- to medium-sized tributary that enters Lake Huron near the town of Bayfield on Highway 21. Although. (in places) it can be a bit tight for casting, the first 10 kilometers of the Bayfield is a nice, moderate-gradient river with lots of boulder-studded runs and pockets. The Bayfield has a decent run of both steelhead and Chinook, and a modest run of coho salmon. Like the Maitland the steelhead run is a mix of wild and stocked fish. It fishes well a day or two after a major freshet, and clears up quicker than the bigger, nearby Maitland. The steelhead season is from the opening of trout season in April to December 31 from Lake Huron to the town of Clinton on Highway 4, which amounts to approximately 15 kilometers of river. The best water for fly fishing is the first 7 or 8 kilometers.

The Bayfield attracts some fishing pressure, but not as much as other Huron streams such as the Nine Mile. Like the Maitland, the Bayfield has some good smallmouth fishing during the summer months.

Recommended Services:

(Refer to Appendix B for addresses and phone numbers.)

The Little Inn of Bayfield

The Little Inn of Bayfield is a quaint historical inn in the town of Bayfield a stone's throw from the Bayfield River. It is a great place for a weekend getaway or a base for fishing area rivers such as the Bayfield, Nine Mile and Maitland rivers. The town of Bayfield has a nice docking facility and many Lake Huron boaters and sailors make their summer base in this quiet little town. Bayfield has numerous craft and art shops in the vicinity of the Little Inn. The food and lodgings at the inn are beyond reproach.

Additionally, the inn hosts fly-fishing weekend schools from time to time.

Grindstone Angling Specialties

Owned and operated by John Valk and Barney Jones in Waterdown, Ontario, Grindstone (905 689-0880) is a full-service dedicated fly shop with a complete stock of flies, fly-tying materials and quality rods, reels and components. John Valk is one of the most well-travelled and knowledgeable guides in Southern Ontario. He is an outspoken conservationist, and has spearheaded many initiatives to improve fishing opportunities and fish populations in the province. His shop in Waterdown also boasts an amply staffed guide service, several of whom I have fished with and found to be knowledgeable and excellent company on the river. Servicing the steelhead and salmon rivers of Lake Huron and Georgian Bay is among their specialties.

Grand Guides Co-op

The Grand Guides Co-op is a guide service based in Kitchener (519-576 2636) that specializes in full-service guiding to fly anglers on the steel-head and salmon rivers of Lake Huron and Georgian Bay and other places, as mentioned in this book.

Karl Vogel

Karl Vogel, a featured guide in *Great Lakes Steelhead*, is, as I have mentioned several places in this book, one of the best steelhead guides and anglers that I have ever met. He specializes in fishing and guiding on the St. Mary's Rapids for steelhead, Atlantic salmon, pink and Chinook salmon. In addition, Karl has access to several beats on the Garden River, a Lake Huron tributary that flows through a First Nations Reserve just east of Sault Ste. Marie. The Garden fishes well for steelhead in the spring and exceptionally well in the fall for Chinook salmon.

Lake Erie Streams

An array of fall steelhead flies
for Southern Ontario streams.

Since the 1930s Lake Erie has been through a multitude of changes. The lake suffered through progressive water quality deterioration up until the 1970s when a multi-national agreement was signed to reduce phosphate levels in Lake Erie. The lake's indigenous population of lake trout and whitefish, and introduced salmonids, had been all but decimated by enormous algae blooms that robbed the lake of oxygen. Within ten years of this agreement the lake responded remarkably, becoming renowned as a walleye and perch hot-bed. Just as this great fishery began perking along nicely the invasion of zebra mussels in the late 80s began. This invasion changed the mesotrophic and even eutrophic water conditions to a clear-water, nutrient-poor situation that resembled the open waters of Lake Superior. At present water visibility in Lake Erie approaches thirty-five feet in some areas. Quite a change from the three-foot visibility conditions during the height of the algae bloom in the 1970s. However nature always seems to adapt, providing good with bad. This clear-water condition now prevalent in the lake, is very desirable for the steelhead population although its not so good for the walleye. Charter boat companies that a few years ago targeted large walleyes are now hooking up routinely with jazzed steelhead in the open waters of Lake Erie. Because of varying depth ranges in the lake, warmwater species and salmonids are seeking out their own niche within this body of water. These factors, combined with the improvements in water quality and spawning habitat within the catchment tributaries of the Grand River and Big Creek, coalesce nicely resulting in a blossoming steelhead fishery. Each year better returns and additional angling opportunities are appearing in these tributary systems. One can only hope that this trend continues.

Most steelhead and salmon found in Ontario's Lake Erie tributaries were originally stocked in U.S. waters (thanks guys!). With the exception of the Grand River, the best return of salmonids occurs in the streams of the Norfolk sand plain in the Long Point Bay area. This large sand plain, in places one-hundred feet deep, acts as a filter system for cool ground water, which in turn makes area tributaries ideal spawning habitat. The streams in the area are sandy, clear and cool, and under favourable conditions fish well for steelhead, salmon and migratory browns.

Lake Erie steelhead average between four and seven pounds when sexually mature, with a number of fish between nine and twelve pounds. Few steelhead exceed this mark, however recently specimens in the fifteen-to twenty-pound class have been reported. Biologists hypothesize that this may be attributed to increasingly favourable forage conditions in the lake (steelhead feed primarily by sight), or the recent introduction of Little Manistee strain steelhead in Ohio (thanks once again). Recently a twenty-six-pound behemoth was boated off the mouth of Big Otter Creek by a downrigging angler.

The prognosis for the steelhead fishery, specifically in the Big Creek and Grand River drainage, is good, and may rival the best fisheries in Ontario in coming years.

Timing for Lake Erie steelhead is similar to most Southern Ontario spring and fall timings. On most streams summer steelhead are as likely as finding a nugget of gold, but on Young Creek, a small, tightly treed, tributary in the Long Point Bay drainage, stray Skamania-strain steelhead surprise unsuspecting brown-trout anglers in July and August each year.

Migratory brown trout in the streams of the Norfolk sand plain are a lot more common than many people realize. These secretive wild browns, reminiscent of sleek-bodied Scottish sea trout, migrate up several area tributaries during the summer months, and in the case of Big Creek, travel 50 kilometers to their

RICK NOVAK

headwater spawning grounds. These browns average five pounds, but many exceed ten, and are likely descendants of the original provincial brown-trout stocking program initiated in 1913. This wild and unique heritage makes it all the more critical to release these handsome fish when caught.

Only a marginal number of Pacific salmon are still stocked in Lake Erie. Most of the runs in Ontario streams are remnant wild populations, providing a decent, fishable number of Chinook and coho salmon in some Long Point Bay tributaries in the fall.

As I mentioned in the introduction to the Lake Huron chapter, obtaining a current road map and fishing regulations is imperative in properly locating and legally fishing the streams mentioned in this chapter.

Fly Patterns

Caddisflies are very important in Lake Erie tributaries, specifically in the Grand River system, which includes Whitemans Creek and the Nith River. Numerous species of caddis thrive in the Grand's nutrient-rich waters, many of which are of the net-spinning variety (see Chapter 11). This is likely why steelhead in this system have a penchant not only for caddis larvae nymph patterns, but skated and dead-drifted caddis dries. Any ardent steelhead-nut will tell you that a steelhead on a dry is bliss; worth five steelhead taken subsurface. Fish Elk Hair Caddis, small Stimulators and steelhead waking dries in these streams when weather and water conditions are mild in May, June and September.

Wet flies, Spey flies and soft hackle patterns are best swung rather than dead-drifted because of the inherent nature of emerging caddisflies. Mayflies are also very important in Grand tributaries such as Whitemans Creek, and size 12 or 10 nymphs from the Hare's Ear family will produce nicely.

On Long Point Bay tributaries like Big Creek, caddis are not quite as important. Subsequently Hare's Ear Nymphs and other general mayfly/stonefly representations will produce well on a dead-drift presentation, as will smallish, subtly coloured egg patterns.

Big Creek

Big Creek is the largest stream flowing into Long Point Bay, and, historically, is the largest producer of steelhead on Lake Erie. The estimated annual return is approximately two-thousand fish.

Big Creek currently has a year-round open season for steelhead in the lowest 40 kilometers of the stream from the village of Lyndoch to the mouth on Long Point Bay; an additional 10-kilometers of extended season water (trout opener in April to December 31) begins at Lyndoch and ends at Highway 3 in Delhi. This top 10 kilometer stretch of Big Creek fishes the best, with an abundance of sandy- and gravely-bottomed riffles, runs and pools that remind you of Michigan's Rifle or Platte rivers. Because the river rarely floods, this forty- to fifty-foot-wide stretch of river is tight with foliage, making the roll cast a valuable angling tool. Below Lyndoch the stream opens up, but takes on a u-shaped, deep channel configuration, which is difficult to read and wade.

The steelhead recovery in this system (which is really a river not a creek) is due to recent instream debris removal and dam modifications by the OMNR and groups such as the Delhi District Anglers Association. Recent electro-fishing studies suggest that steelhead juveniles have increased dramatically in this system, and may even double the return in the not-too-distant future.

Migratory browns are also available in Big Creek during their annual summer migration. They can also be successfully pursued by "flats fishing" the mouths of Long Point Bay rivers with a sink-tip line and a lake pattern such as a Clouser Deep Minnow.

Grand River

The Grand is best known for its brown-trout fishery in the Fergus/Elora area, and is thoroughly covered in Chapter 11. However, this very large river system is becoming more and more important for steelhead angling as dam and water conditions improve and make upstream spawning grounds accessible and suitable.

The Grand River is approximately 200 kilometers long. The City of Brantford, situated at the half-way point, separates two distinctly differing sections of river. The lower section, below Brantford, is primarily clay-bottomed impervious soil that is not suitable for salmonid production, but very suitable and productive for smallmouth bass, mooneye, garpike and other warmwater species. Above Brantford, the dominant nature of the watershed is very suitable for salmonid reproduction, with an abundance of sand and gravel deposits and natural upwellings of ground water. Until the late 1980s this productive habitat was inaccessible to steelhead and salmon because Lorne Dam in Brantford blocked passage. The dam was removed in 1989 and this has been a boon to the steelhead population in the Grand and her tributaries. Dams at Dunnville (6 kilometers upstream of Lake Erie) and at Brantford (Wilkes Dam) are cleared easily by steelhead. The Caledonia Dam, located 50 kilometers from the lake, delays steelhead somewhat during low, high, or cold flows, subsequently fish stack in this region making it a good place to fish. This section of river along Highway 54 south of the community of Caledonia, is nice water to fly fish, albeit somewhat murky with clay deposits and algae at certain times in the spring and fall. The section of river south of Brantford offers clearer water conditions with lots of open space for fly rodding in broad runs, riffles and delicious-looking pools, perfect for swinging a soft-hackle or drifting a caddis dry.

Just recently the Grand River from the mouth to 25 kilometers downstream of the Wilkes Dam in Brantford has been approved for an extended season for browns and steelhead (from October 1 to December 31). A conservative possession limit of one fish should prevent overharvest.

Like most Southern Ontario streams the Grand receives both spring and fall run steelhead; however, the fall run seems to have a higher than normal percentage of early fish, which makes this river very significant for dry-fly steelheaders. Steelhead usually make an appearance below Caledonia by Labour Day.

Whitemans Creek

A few kilometers upstream of Wilkes Dam in Brantford on the Grand enters Whitemans Creek. It is primarily known for resident trout fishing as covered in Chapter 12. Again, because of the removal of Lorne Dam in 1989, Whitemans now receives a growing number of Lake Erie steelhead. Whitemans boasts an artificial-only, catch-and-release stretch known as App's Mill Nature Centre, between Robinson Road and Cleaver Sideroad. An area renowned for excellent mayfly hatches, primarily Hendricksons and sulphers.

This section is a small (forty- to fifty-foot wide), pretty stream with lots of gravel bars and sweeping bends that make fly fishing a pleasure. It is also great spawning habitat for steelhead and subsequently is closed to angling from October 1 to the beginning of trout season (last Saturday in April). A good opportunity for both fresh and drop-back steelhead occurs after the trout opener in this stretch of Whitemans, and continues for approximately two weeks during most years.

Nith River

The Nith is another tributary of the Grand, the confluence of which occurs in the town of Paris, about 125 kilometers upstream of Lake Erie. Like the main Grand and Whitemans, the Nith and her tributaries now engender wild steelhead as a direct result of the destruction of Lorne Dam and augmented water qualities. The river is moderate in size and nicely navigated with a canoe. The region encompassed by the Village of Ayr and Paris (just south of the 401 freeway on Highway 50) is particularly inviting with a pleasant riffle, run, pool mixture. This stretch, however, can run quite turbid after a good rain due to the intensive agricultural activities in this area. Fishing regulations at present do not allow fall angling, similar to Whitemans Creek.

The Nith is blessed with a great smallmouth bass fishery in its lower reaches.

Recommended Services:

(Refer to Chapter 2: Lake Huron Streams and Appendix B)

Lake Ontario Streams

Bob McKenzie with a wild Lake Ontario steelhead.

RICK NOVAK

Lake Ontario is the smallest of the Great Lakes, but conversely produces the biggest steelhead and salmon. If you are after a twenty-pound-class steelhead, or a thirty-pound Chinook, turn to the tributaries of Lake Ontario—and test your knots.

Lake Ontario's historic indigenous fish community originally included lake trout, whitefish, and the king of all game fish—the Atlantic salmon. These fish thrived in the deep and productive waters of Lake Ontario until they were decimated by overharvest, habitat degradation and the indiscriminate damming of spawning tributaries. During Lake Ontario's heyday, Atlantics ran all of her tributaries except for the Niagara. The runs of Atlantics in the now-urbanized Greater Toronto streams, such as the Don, Credit and Humber, were remarkable, as was the harvest. At present the Atlantic salmon restoration program continues to plug away at attempting to re-establish these wonderful fish, with marginal results. We're hoping the new strategy of introducing Atlantic salmon fry to stream sections that are not heavily utilized by steelhead will improve the results.

In addition to these encouraging stocking efforts, Toronto-area OMNR fish and wildlife biologist, Mark Heaton, informs that some significant stream improvements are now underway to improve urbanized streams, such as the Don and Humber rivers in the Metropolitan Toronto area. This will benefit both anadromous fish and the resident brown-trout population, which is particularly healthy in the Humber River. A fishway on the East Humber River in Richmond Hill is scheduled for completion in 1999. Collectively these improvements could make for some incredible urban fishing, considering that Toronto is one of the largest cities in North America.

Steelhead, first introduced to Lake Ontario in 1878, continue to thrive and have established remarkable wild returns in many Lake Ontario tributaries. Wilmot Creek, for example, receives a run of approximately 10,000 steelhead, even though this stream is only 40 feet wide near the lake. Lake Ontario steelhead average between eight and ten pounds; a fish in the high teens attracts some attention, while fish exceeding the twenty-pound mark are worthy of trophy recognition.

Lake Ontario's Canadian tributaries can be divided into two distinct categories: ones that drain the Niagara Escarpment west of Toronto, and those that drain the Oak Ridges Moraine east of this mega-city. The eastern streams are better in terms of water conditions, size of returns, and numbers of wild fish. The Oak Ridges Moraine drainage has sandy, well-forested headwaters with abundant ground water of limestone origin. These streams run clear and cold, and relatively stable. They have predominant sand and gravel conditions for spawning, and deep undercut banks and flotsam for juvenile survival. In brief, they are steelhead factories. With the exception of stocking programs on Duffins and Oshawa creeks, the steelhead running in this drainage system are wild. Duffins, Oshawa, Bowmanville, Wilmot and Shelter Valley creeks, and the Ganaraska River, are streams of the Oak Ridges Moraine covered in this chapter.

The streams of the Niagara Escarpment catchment, west of Toronto, are stocked with steelhead, but still maintain wild returns of approximately fifty percent. The headwaters of these streams (Bronte Creek, Credit River, and Rouge River) are of cool, ground-water origin and provide good spawning habitat. However, as these rivers approach urbanized areas near the lake, they deteriorate in water quality and temperature. Nevertheless, they receive excellent runs of steelhead (and Chinook salmon) and provide a great doorstep fishery for the highest-populated urban area in Canada. It is obviously important to preserve this condition.

According to Jim Bowlby, ardent fly-angler and regional biologist for the OMNR, the top five steelhead producers on the Canadian side of Lake Ontario are the Credit and Ganaraska rivers, and the Bowmanville, Shelter Valley and Wilmot creeks. Obviously these streams are your best bets for angling during the spring and fall steelhead runs.

Chinook salmon, which run the tributaries of both drainages, are the mainstay of the offshore boat fishery in Lake Ontario. They also provide ample fly angling opportunity in September and October in these tributaries, and attract egg-feeding steelhead into the rivers behind them. Lake Ontario's rivers (in particular the Ganaraska and the Wilmot) sustain wild populations of Chinook that may produce 400,000 smolts annually.

Coho salmon were stocked heavily in the 70s and 80s, discontinued in the early 90s, and recently reintroduced on request of the angling public. It seems coho runs provide a viable late November, early December fishery in Lake Ontario streams. Coho are known for their eagerness to take a fly and their inherent zip, even in very cold water.

Brown trout are stocked heavily around marinas, docks and river-mouths—particularly on the west end of the lake—and create a good spring and fall shoreline fishery for wading fly rodders. Unlike the svelte denizens of Lake Erie, these fish are football-shaped lunkers that exceed ten pounds and often attain sizes in excess of thirty pounds. Likely due to their portly physique, they do not run considerable distances up Lake Ontario tributaries, and should be pursued close to the mouth in September in streams like the Ganaraska, Wilmot, Rouge, Oshawa and Bronte. These streams receive decent numbers of stocked browns that are planted along the Lake Ontario shore primarily to create a fall shoreline fishery.

Lake Ontario tributaries are not quite as long as other Southern Ontario tributaries, such as the Grand in Lake Erie's drainage or the Maitland and the Saugeen of Lake Huron; but they certainly provide salmonids with considerable river miles to run and provide angling opportunity. They are of similar nature with respect to the agricultural regions through which they flow, and similarly cloud up quickly after a good rainfall. In general, however, they are small enough to clear within a short period of time, varying between eight and forty-eight hours.

Once again, it will be necessary for you to utilize a good road map and current fishing regulations before you set out to conquer these streams. More so than anywhere else in the province, you will be dealing with private land, which must be respected. Serious anglers that frequent these prolific Lake Ontario steelhead and salmon rivers should consider joining a private fishing club to access the best rivers with the least angling pressure. At the time of this writing, the open seasons and possession limits for steelhead on Lake Ontario tributaries is being reviewed, and hopefully enhanced fishing opportunities and lower harvest limits will be the result of these talks.

Fly Patterns

The Niagara Escarpment streams mentioned in this chapter (Bronte, Credit and Rouge) have good populations of stoneflies and mayflies in their headwaters. Subsequently, steelhead returning to these rivers should recognize a nicely presented stonefly or mayfly nymph as something that resembles dinner. Mike's Stone is a simple, workable stonefly pattern that will produce, as will the ubiquitous G.R. Hare's Ear nymph. I would go with a sharp, strong hook, such as a TMC or Daiichi, in sizes 12, 10 and 8. Water conditions will dictate tippet size. Go with the

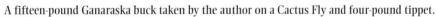

A fifteen-pound Ganaraska buck taken by the author on a Cactus Fly and four-pound tippet.

Bob McKenzie beaches a good steelhead on the Ganaraska River.

plantings. In the Bronte above Lowville are some decent populations of resident browns and brook trout. The Bronte Creek Provincial Park area, between Highway 5 and the Queen Elizabeth Way, is also a popular spot for steelhead and salmon fly anglers. Both the Lowville section and the Provincial Park section are fairly small with tight pools and runs that are conducive to short-line nymphing.

Bronte Creek has several sections of water with varying seasons; including a year-round fish sanctuary, and some water that is open to angling year-round near the mouth of Lake Ontario. Be sure to check your fishing regulations carefully before angling and respect private property.

Although I have never fished the Bronte under optimum conditions, I found this river interesting enough to hold my attention for several hours of afternoon fishing in both spring and fall. The Bronte is of special importance to fly anglers interested in dancing with big Chinook on fairly light tackle in September and October. The Bronte is also a good spot for migratory browns in September.

Credit River

The Credit River is the epitome of the classic angling opportunity in an urban setting. The lower stretch of this prolific steelhead and salmon stream flows through the City of Mississauga, a heavily populated community which to an outsider is really an extension of Toronto. The Credit is a must-fish stream for those travellers that frequent Toronto on business, being only a fifteen-minute drive from Pearson International Airport in Toronto (in moderate traffic anyway). There is a section of river open year-round south of the Q.E.W. and also north of Highway 5. The latter of which fishes best for the fly angler, and offers a great opportunity for a steelhead even during mild days in the dead of winter. I have personally fished the Erindale Park section of the Credit (right in the City of Mississauga off Burnamthorpe Road) numerous times and have thoroughly enjoyed the experience each time. This is a medium-sized stream that averages fifty to one-hundred feet in width with a nice rifle-run-pool character that makes it ideal for either swinging a wet fly or high-stick nymphing. I have fished this river during moderately clear flows in the fall and in turbid conditions in early spring with good results. The key of course is to hit the Credit with just the right amount of flow and clarity, which generally occurs just after a moderate rainfall. The Credit boasts good runs of large Chinook and the large steelhead Lake Ontario is famous for producing.

When fishing the Credit you will encounter several other anglers, especially when the word gets out that a good run is in the river. Many of these anglers will be fishing float rigs: that is long rods in the twelve-foot range with large float reels (resembling fly reels) loaded with monofilament and a small float with either a roe bag or a nymph imitation at the terminal end. This technique is deadly effective for making presentations to prime lies on medium- and large- sized rivers.

The last time I fished the Credit River for steelhead while researching this book was in the spring of 1998. The water was fairly high and turbid due to a good rain a few days previous. The water had cleared to fishable levels but was still considerably high. While watching float anglers effectively working mid-stream slicks and pockets I considered the limitations of my standard 9-1/2 foot rod and wished I had packed a Spey rod. In my humble opinion, the Credit (and many other medium- to large-sized Southern Ontario steelhead streams) is an ideal place for using a Spey rod. Spey rods enable you to present a fly at considerable distances with little room for a backcast, and, more importantly, enable you to keep your fly line off the water when presenting a nymph or egg pattern near the bottom in prime lies.

Whatever rod and method you prefer, however, the Credit can pay big dividends to anglers who take the time to spend a few hours fishing this urban gem. I recently told my good friend Bruce Miller about the

largest-sized tippet you can to facilitate proper and quick handling of Lake Ontario's jumbo steelhead. On sunny days with clear water conditions you may have to go to a durable four-pound tippet to get takes. I managed to land a fifteen-pound buck steelhead on the Ganaraska on four-pound Scientific Anglers tippet, although I'm sure there was some divine intervention involved in this angling feat.

Oak Ridges Moraine streams, such as the Ganaraska, have dominant populations of caddis and mayflies. Subsequently stonefly patterns are not as important here; although still workable. Caddis larvae nymphs should be carried by the bushel.

Egg/attractor patterns in conservative sizes (12 through 8) also dupe Lake Ontario steelhead and salmon. The Nympho, a jazzed-up version of the Hare's Ear nymph that I developed, works remarkably well in Lake Ontario rivers. I'm still tying these for friends in the South after hooking several steelhead on them during my research sojourns.

Bronte Creek

Bronte Creek is a medium-sized stream about fifty to sixty feet wide nearest the lake. Although it has good groundwater sources, it resembles a spate river in the lower reaches where most of the angling for migratories is done. This is due to the prevalence of bedrock and urbanization in this area. Similar to true spate rivers, the runs of steelhead and salmon in the Bronte hinge on rainfall. When flows are decent the Bronte receives good runs of steelhead, Chinook, coho and brown trout. The Lowville Park area, north of Highway 5 near Waterdown, Ontario, fishes well for steelhead and Chinook, and has been the site of some Atlantic salmon

Credit and suggested he pack his fly gear the next time he had business in Toronto. He took me up on this advice one October afternoon, and although he didn't hit pay dirt himself, he watched a local river faithful land a chrome twelve-pound steelhead. He also spent a good hour talking to another regular about the best flies and techniques for the river, and got a bang out of being able to buy a hot dog and cold soda from a streamside vendor that mused, "Business is slow—can't wait for a good run to come in."

Rouge River

The Rouge River is a Lake Ontario tributary that flows through the Toronto suburb of Scarborough, and has been the site of some recent stream restoration efforts by a number of groups, including the Metro East Anglers, Ontario Streams, Rouge Park and the Ministry of Natural Resources. The Rouge is a freestone river with some amazing pools and riffles. The main branch of the river averages about thirty feet in width and flows through the scenic Rouge River Valley. The Rouge offers some good fly-fishing opportunities for steelhead, Chinook salmon and brown trout from Highway 48 in Markham to Lake Ontario a distance of approximately 25 kilometers. The Little Rouge River—a branch of the main Rouge—offers some good opportunities from Highway 402 upstream to 19th Avenue near the village of Dixon Hill (an additional 20-kilometer stretch).

A fishway at Milne Reservoir in Markham, due for completion in late 1999, will make another 50 kilometers of stream accessible to steelhead and their followers.

All this adds up to some attractive steelhead and salmon fishing on the Rouge.

The Rouge River has several access points, including a number of parking areas in Rouge Park, the largest urban park in Canada.

Bob McKenzie with a Ganaraska buck steelhead
taken on a Gold Ribbed Hare's Ear Nymph.steelhead.

Duffins Creek

Duffins Creek flows into Lake Ontario at the community of Ajax, east of Toronto. Below Highway 401 this tributary averages 30 to 40 feet in width; above the 401 the creek divides into an east and west branch and both of these are about 25 feet wide. Duffins, like other Oak Ridges Moraine tributaries, has a decent run of steelhead. In addition it receives a good run of stocked browns from nearby harbours in the lower reaches of the river.

Duffins is less urbanized than the Rouge and subsequently is less effected by heavy rains, having a much more stable flow. This makes the surrounding foliage a little tighter to the bank on Duffins. For this reason, a lot of fly anglers find the stretch of water from the confluence downstream more conducive to their sport.

Duffins Creek also has a respectable brook trout population in its headwaters.

Oshawa Creek

As its name would suggest the Oshawa Creek is located in the City of Oshawa on Highway 401. Similar to Duffins Creek there exists two branches of the stream that join together prior to entering Lake Ontario. Both branches offer steelhead, Chinook salmon and brown trout opportunities for the fly angler.

Oshawa Creek has a reputation of being especially productive after a good rain.

Bowmanville Creek

This is a great stream to learn how to fly fish for steelhead. The Bowmanville has a nice composition of riffles, runs and pools that can be read and fished quite easily. There are a number of sandy, undercut banks and log jams that provide cover for migrating steelhead and salmon. The best water for fly fishing generally speaking is between the Village of Hampton on Tonton Road and the mouth of the river just south of the Town of Bowmanville on Lake Ontario. There are two conservation areas well worth spending some time exploring: one off Highway 2 and another on Jackman Road. The latter has water with slightly better gradient and a more freestone character than the lower, sandy section of the stream near Highway 2.

Soper Creek, north of the community of Bowmanville, is a tributary of the Bowmanville Creek that also fishes well for steelhead despite its smaller size. Both Soper and Bowmanville Creek have good populations of resident brown trout that can be targeted between spring and fall steelhead runs.

Wilmot Creek

Considering the moderate size of Wilmot Creek it boasts a tremendous spring run of steelhead (over 10,000 fish) and some nice fly-fishing conditions. Wilmot Creek enters Lake Ontario just west of Newcastle, and is the next fishing stop between Bowmanville Creek and the Ganaraska River. A parking lot off Highway 2 provides easy access to a provincial fishing area on both sides of that highway. This is nice fly-fishing water; the river averages about thirty feet wide, but there is ample room for a backcast in most places.

Much of the upstream reaches of Wilmot Creek flow through private property and permission must be obtained to fish these areas.

The provincial section below Highway 2 is a good place to encounter migratory browns in September.

Ganaraska River

The Ganie', as she is affectionately referred to by those that love this stream, is one of Ontario's greatest steelhead streams. In fact, I experienced the best fly fishing for steelhead in my life on the Ganie'. Rivaled in numbers of steelhead by only Wilmot Creek, the Ganaraska receives in excess of 10,000 steelhead during the spring run. One can come to grips with the magnitude of this run by standing below the fishway on the Corbett Dam in the town of Port Hope and watching the incredible

A Ganaraska steelhead taken on a Hex Nymph.

numbers of steelhead lining up below the dam and jumping up into the fishway (understandably a fish sanctuary). Below the sanctuary to the mouth of the river on Lake Ontario is where the biggest steelhead in the province are caught each year. Numerous steelhead in excess of twenty pounds spawn in this lower stretch of the river rather than trek through the bedrock shallows and the upstream dam and fishway. It goes without saying that this stretch of river also gets a tremendous run of anglers, but if you're intent on a big silver steelhead, this is the place. The best bet to avoid crowds here would be to fish during absolute tough weather—when only the grittiest of die-hards fish this stretch.

Above the fishway is a substantial stretch of river that flows through rich farmland. There are numerous places to access the Ganaraska along country roads but many of these are posted, private property. Some research and planning, and polite inquiries, can result in opportunities on private water. There are also a number of stretches that are leased by private clubs, and if one is really serious about fishing the Ganaraska without the crowds this would be the best avenue to pursue.

I was lucky enough to fish some private water on the Ganaraska with Sage rod representative, Bob McKenzie, of Oshawa. We fished two nice stretches of river both during and after a heavy spring rain. In the morning, while the rain poured down on our heads, we had a number of hook-ups with steelhead until the river became so muddy that poor visibility made fly fishing fruitless. We returned the next morning and fished the entire day as the river cleared progressively as the day went on. Surprisingly, by evening the river was very clear and the fish were once again quite skittish, but during the middle phases of this clearing process, I hooked and landed more steelhead than I could imagine. In fact I lost count. And

as evening approached I purposefully took apart my rod and stowed away my reel so that I would have to stop fishing and take a rest. I landed several typical Lake Ontario steelhead in the eight- to twelve-pound class, a couple of fish in the low teens and a big, bad and dark male that likely went in the neighbourhood of fifteen.

This was an interesting experience. Early in the day, when the river was still quite turbid with runoff, the flies that produced the best were bright egg/attractor patterns like the Cactus Fly and the Nympho. As the day progressed and the water cleared, the fish began to disdain these patterns so I dug some natural-looking nymphs out of my trout box and continued to dupe big steelhead. In the low-light conditions of late evening I fished some more private water farther upstream and hooked both drop-backs and fresh fish that were moving through some shallow runs just downstream of prime spawning beds. I actually observed several steelhead open their mouths and take my nymph in the clear, shallow water. This was important for me to observe, as I have often heard steelhead anglers say that these fish do not feed on nymphs during their spawning runs, and most hook-ups by fly anglers occur by inadvertently "lining" fish: that is drifting the leader through their mouths and then setting the hook into the side of their head. Clearly observing these fish open their mouths and suck in my nymph pattern blew that myth out of the water. In steelhead fishing there are a lot of opinions, and one thing is for sure, opinions are like brains: everybody has one!

In addition to these memorable steelhead runs, the Ganaraska boasts big runs of Lake Ontario Chinook salmon, some in excess of thirty pounds. Like many other streams in this region, the Ganie' is also a good bet for migratory brown trout.

Shelter Valley Creek

Shelter Valley Creek is situated just east of Cobourg. This medium-sized Lake Ontario tributary boasts a rather large run of steelhead in the 5,000 range. It fishes well with fly-fishing techniques, but similar to other area streams, such as the Ganaraska, there is a lot of posted water. There are, however, some areas where you can access private sections of river for a price, a pay-as-you-play situation you might say. But the fishing can be worth a few dollars on Shelter Valley Creek when the run is at full steam.

Niagara River

The Niagara River is really a tributary of Lake Ontario in a class unto itself. This is a big, brawling tributary that commands the ultimate respect from both the walking and boating angler. Only one river in Ontario rivals the magnitude of the Niagara, and that is the Nipigon River on the north shore of Superior. The Niagara, however, is bigger and forms the waterway between Lake Erie and Lake Ontario. And, of course, is the river that flows over world-renowned Niagara Falls.

For many years the Niagara was not considered a targetable river for fly anglers due to its size and depth. However, fly-angling pioneers such as Rick Kustich from New York state, have used modern technology—and a lot of down-home ingenuity—to master this magnificent river. Some of the techniques are less than classic, but necessary. Like steelheading anywhere in the Great Lakes Basin, ninety percent of your hook-ups are near the bottom. And in a deep, fast river like the Niagara, this can pose a problem for fly anglers.

Basically there are two approaches, both with inherent advantages and disadvantages: high-stick nymphing with a floating line and a long, twelve-foot-plus leader, and swinging a streamer or wet fly on a heavy sink-tip or lead-core line.

Rick Kustich with a big Niagara River steelhead.

High-stick nymphing on the lower Niagara produces well in the spring when fish are close to spawning areas, and also in the late fall when water temperatures are colder and the steelhead are in the river in good numbers. Little room for back-casts is afforded by the walls of the gorge, and wading is virtually impossible in most cases. Subsequently a long rod is a favoured tool, and a two-handed Spey rod is the ultimate for flipping out long roll casts. Heavy split shot is necessary for getting the system down to the bottom, and egg flies, including the ubiquitous Glow Bug in various shades of pink, orange and peach, are good producers on the Niagara.

Streamers and wets swung on sink-tips produce well in moderate water temperatures, such as those found in May and through most of the fall, when steelhead, salmon, lake trout and brown trout are encountered in the Niagara. Because the Niagara is fed by tepid Lake Erie, temperatures remain favourable for swinging a Spey fly or a streamer well into December. Fall steelhead are especially aggressive in the Niagara River. Swinging streamers is best done from a boat on the Niagara; more of the river is accessible to the fly angler, and backcast room is not in short supply. Caution is a necessity when boating this mighty river, and most river aficionados recommend nothing smaller than a 16-foot boat powered by a twenty-horse motor.

When scheduling an outing on the Niagara consider the following: spring fishing picks up in late April when the ice from Lake Erie clears from the river. Steelhead are found in the largest numbers during the spring run in late April and early May. During the summer months the water temperatures rise in the gorge and fly anglers turn to smallmouth bass fishing in the Niagara. Beginning in late August, Chinook salmon begin filtering into the river, with the best numbers entering the river in late September and into October. When the Chinook run begins to taper off in late October steelhead become prevalent in the river, reaching their fall peak in numbers by mid-November. This is a great time to fish the river for feisty fall steelhead that can often reach the fifteen-pound mark. Lake trout in the ten- to twelve-pound category are also fairly common catches in the Niagara in October and November, and also in April, May and June. Brown trout are also encountered during the fall—some of which can exceed twenty pounds!

Access points for the lower Niagara include a boat launch at the Queenston sand docks just downstream of the Queenston/Lewiston Bridge (good walk-and-wade access and boat access); the Whirlpool parking lot and stairs off the Niagara Parkway (walk-and-wade only), or the stairs into the gorge from the park at the general store at the top of the hydro road (also accessed from the Niagara Parkway).

Water levels in the gorge can change without notice depending on hydroelectric demands. In addition, although the water conditions are generally clear or slightly off-colour, the river can run turbid after a good windstorm on Lake Erie. Often, as Rick Kustich explains, when the river is running slightly off-colour, steelhead and salmon tend to hold closer to the bank and are thus within reach of the fly angler.

Even walk-and-wade anglers should consider either a floater coat, or an inflatable vest when fishing the Niagara. No fish is worth your life.

Boat anglers should consider obtaining both a New York and an Ontario fishing license to legally access waters on both sides of the Canada-U.S. border.

Recommended Services:

(Refer Appendix B for addresses and phone numbers)

Grindstone Angling Specialties

Grindstone's guides service Lake Ontario steelhead and salmon tributaries, including the Niagara River.

Hudson Bay and James Bay Streams

A view from the bow on the mighty Winisk River.

RICK NOVAK

Along Ontario's 1,210-kilometer Hudson and James Bay shoreline there are numerous remote streams—some large and some very large—that for the most part are inaccessible to fly anglers. Unless you have your own reliable float plane, there is no such thing as venturing out on your own and exploring new rivers unguided. In fact you must rely almost exclusively on outfitters and guide services that have established themselves in certain areas that are serviced by the few small communities in the far north. There are many areas that do not have such services. These area streams are fished little, if ever, and their species content have not even been catalogued by biologists.

However on the rivers that host lodges and guide services, the experience available on these pristine flows is unforgettable. Although in some of the most northern rivers, arctic char and grayling are available to the fly angler, the premier species in this watershed is the brook trout. Big and abundant brook trout. Available in a true wilderness surrounding that in itself is worth the time, planning and air-fare involved in reaching these very northern points. On my first trip to a Hudson Bay tributary (the Winisk River), I found myself immediately awestruck by the vastness and beauty of my surroundings. Everywhere I looked I saw something worth photographing. Indeed during my six-day trip I snapped off eight rolls of 36 exposure film and wished I had more. I caught numerous brook trout over the eighteen-inch mark, with several incidental catches of walleye and northern pike. The fish were eager biters—not having been subjected to much fishing pressure—and fought valiantly in the Winisk's powerful currents.

Another more subtle bonus was the knowledge I gained from the native river guides that craftily guided our party safely through 200 kilometers of untethered river. This knowledge was not only of the river and of the fish, but of the native culture itself. We fished pools that had been producing fish for the sustenance of native families for generations. We learned of edible and useful plants; everything from wild mint (in case you forgot the Crest) to damp moss for cleaning your hands. We watched in awe as our guides tacked and scampered their twenty-foot motorized canoes through deadly-looking rapids with expert precision. These northern tributaries are a place to catch trophy trout, and take a look back in time, into an almost forgotten way of life.

Unlike the Great Lakes tributaries, which in most cases are relatively short and have even shorter lengths of stream accessible to migratory fish, the streams of Hudson and James Bays are extremely long and have numerous subsidiary tributaries. Of the rivers that are serviced by outfitters and guide services, the best fly fishing is afforded by the streams that are medium sized. Several guiding services are now offering fly-fishing trips and tailor their packages to fit the needs of the fly angler. Most native operations guide on several different streams, and rotate parties to prevent undue fishing pressure on any given stretch of river, and to ensure a quality angling experience. As the harvest of fish for sustenance is part of the native culture, you may wish to advise your guide upon booking that you are only interested in catch and release or minimal harvest if in fact that is your desire. It is also wise to book a party that consists exclusively of fly anglers. Mixed parties are often difficult to manage for the guide as fly fishing and spin fishing dictate different water types and other special considerations.

Fly Patterns

Similar to other large brook trout haunts, such as the Nipigon River and Nipigon Bay streams, large baitfish imitations produce the best results on these northern tributaries. Rabbit-strip patterns, such as the Zonker and the Butt Monkey series, produce good results in sizes 2 and 4. Tie your patterns with red, orange or chartreuse as secondary colours, under natural-coloured browns and olives. Gold flash is also a good addition to realistic-coloured baitfish patterns. Muddler Minnows, Mickey Finns and Gray Ghosts are good traditional patterns to carry. As for dries and nymphs, consider that stoneflies are a large and well-represented food source for large brook trout in these areas. The

The late Emmanuel Jacob was instrumental in promoting fly fishing on the Winisk system.

George Ozburn with a typical Winisk River brook trout.

Kaufmann Stimulator series of stonefly dries should be carried in sizes 12 through 6 in yellow and orange. Any stonefly nymph pattern will suffice for subsurface presentations. Keep in mind that most of your fishing will likely be presenting large streamers on a sink-tip line using the wet-fly swing technique.

Special Considerations

Like anywhere in Northern Ontario, mosquitoes and black flies are a reality in the far north of the province. In fact, the farther north you go the worse they get, so it pays to come prepared when you travel. I should stress that you must avoid developing a paranoia about "the bugs." Simply come prepared for them both in attitude and equipment: people have lived happily dealing with insects in many parts of the world since the beginning of time. As for equipment, insect repellent is a must anytime between May and September. Bring a supply containing Deet for your face and neck, and a repellent such as Citronella for your hands. Deet repellents, however effective, are detrimental to fly lines and leaders and should not come into contact with your hands. Head-nets are an option for walk-and-wade fishing along tributaries where the effects of wind do not abate the insects. A medium-weight sleeping bag will suffice for unheated cabins and tents. Pack conservatively, but ensure that you have at least two pairs of durable, quick-drying, cotton, long-sleeve shirts and cargo pants. Polypropylene underwear and socks, combined with fleece tops and bottoms, will keep you warm and dry during inclement weather (it can snow even in June), or during extended periods of wading. At the other extreme, temperatures can reach 75 or 80 degrees, so sunscreen and a wide-brimmed hat are also necessities.

Winisk River

The Winisk is a major tributary of Hudson Bay in Ontario's far north. It flows 450 kilometers from the Ojibwa village of Webequie to Hudson

Bay, where at one time the town of Winisk was situated at the mouth of this powerful river. That is until the effects of a record spring thaw lifted the ice flows, and like giant bulldozers, literally pushed the town far out into the sea. The present day town of Winisk is now wisely situated several miles west of its former location.

The headwaters of the river near Webequie is very lake-like in nature, ranging from one to two kilometers in width. Once you begin travelling northward, however, the river begins to look like what typifies so many of the Hudson and James Bay tributaries—large thundering rapids separated by long solemn stretches of quiet water.

I had the good fortune of fishing the Winisk with the late Emmanuel Jacob, former operator of Winisk River Camps in Webequie. Good fortune not only to be shown where the brook trout haunts and hideouts were, but also good fortune to be guided by expert rivermen on a wild and untethered river that would make short work of the sturdiest of craft with one small navigational error. The long churning rapids of the Winisk—in places 100 yards wide and 400 yards long—are no place for the general pleasure-boating public. Emmanuel's team of guides have all completed a four-year apprenticeship on the Winisk prior to being allowed to guide clients solo. Need I say more.

Tragically, Emmanual was killed in a house fire on January 17, 1998. Emmanual, always a gentleman and a true leader, was instrumental in bringing fly-fishing technology to his guide service, and introducing native culture to his clients.

At first, like all large rivers, the Winisk is overwhelming to say the least. But as I have consistently experienced with all large rivers, if you dissect the flow into smaller, more manageable sections, you can

effectively read and fish the water. The best place to accomplish this—and not so coincidentally the best place to catch brook trout—is near rapids and falls, which are very numerous on the Winisk. Wye Rapids, Baskineig Falls and Seashell Rapids are all major sections of the river that are notably good fly-fishing waters.

I found that large, natural-coloured, rabbit-strip flies with bright orange and chartreuse marabou underwings worked very well in the tannic-stained waters of the Winisk. The biggest concentrations of brookies seemed to be below large rapids and falls, where obviously they were feeding on the abundance of aquatic life churning in current seams and back-eddies. On a particularly spectacular afternoon at Baskineig Falls I hooked a dozen brookies in one hour, and witnessed several other members of our party experiencing the same kind of fishing. The brook trout seemed all to be in the 16- to 18-inch category.

A couple of invaluable tips for fishing the Winisk:

•Try casting a heavy sink-tip line (like Scientific Anglers 13-foot Steelhead V) two line weights heavier than your rod designation (i.e. 8-weight line on a 6-weight rod). Modern day fast-action graphite rods will load and perform much better in windy conditions if you use a heavier-rated line.

•The second tip is true on the Winisk as it is on any brook-trout water, and that is once the brook trout stop taking a certain pattern during an apparent feeding frenzy, try changing the pattern drastically and you will hook additional fish. Often you may assume that you have hooked all the eager biters in the run, but for some reason if you switch patterns you can increase your luck.

Winisk River Camps caters to fly-fishing parties by targeting more suitable stretches of water for fly angling. If water conditions are

Winisk River guide Isaiah Jacob runs a set of heavy rapids.

A walleye from the Winisk taken on a Strip Leech.

suitable, tributary streams such as the Frog, Croal and Ashweig Rivers, can be productive waters. These streams are not near as large as the Winisk, and subsequently are not as foreboding to the fly angler. Additionally, the Camp fishes many of these streams on an annual rotating basis to minimize fishing pressure on any particular stretch of water.

Winisk River Camps operates three camps on the Winisk River, two on the Ashweig River, and one on each of the Frog and the Croal. A typical camp consists of a guest cabin, a guide cabin, a cookhouse and an icehouse (and of course a quaint little backhouse).

The best timing for brook trout fishing is between June 1 and September 15.

Sutton River

The Sutton River is situated much farther north than the Winisk, in close proximity to Hudson Bay. Nearby Polar Bear Provincial Park on the south shore of Hudson Bay is a denning area for polar bears, which is an added bonus for the fly angler equipped with a good camera and a *high-powered* zoom lens. Fishing the Sutton system provides the opportunity for both resident and sea-run brook trout; with the latter entering the river system during the last week of July and the first week of August. This is also the best time for catching the migration of polar bears to this area of the shore. Both sea-run and resident fish range in the 3- to 6-pound category. The Sutton River is serviced by Albert's Fishing Camp and Wabusk Expeditions, both situated in Peawanuck Ontario and accessible by float plane from Webequie (Winisk River) or Hearst, Ontario. Both Albert's Fishing Camp and Wabusk Expeditions have base camps on Sutton Lake, a fifty-kilometer long, narrow lake that forms the headwaters of the Sutton River in the Sutton Ridges—a high point of land in the far north. The lake is inhabited by lake trout, northern pike and brook trout; however the best fly-fishing opportunity is in the Sutton River, which flows from the lake another 120 kilometers north to Hudson Bay. The river has a moderate flow and is easily wadeable in most places. Although some angling is done from canoes, the majority of fly fishing is done by wading into the river and working pools and deep runs. The river has a good population of giant stoneflies (*Pteronarcys*); subsequently stonefly nymph patterns in sizes 2, 4 and 6 work well anywhere on the river. The brookies will also take large dries, such as Sofa pillows and Stimulators, and particularly Muddlers tied with large heads and waked on the surface. In addition, these brookies will pounce on any mouse pattern twitched near a grassy bank.

Quite often fish from Hudson Bay can be seen moving up through the shallows. They are identical in appearance to resident fish, except the fresh-run brook trout from the salt have a more silvery hue to them, similar to coaster brook trout from Lake Superior. Both resident and sea-run brookies run from 2 to 6 pounds, with the average fish being approximately 3 pounds. There have been brook trout caught over the 6-pound mark, with the largest being a stunning 9 1/2-pounder. This behemoth came from the gorge between Sutton and Hawley Lakes; the latter being an extension of Sutton Lake, but for all intents and purposes this is all the same watershed. Fly anglers can routinely experience twenty- to thirty-fish days on the Sutton.

All told there is about 160 kilometers of pristine wilderness to be seen and fished when on the Sutton. Some groups wish to float the entire stretch and get picked up by a float plane at Hudson Bay. This is about 8 kilometers north of the tree-line in the Canadian tundra; an area known for nesting geese and other waterfowl, and as I mentioned before, polar bears. The bears do not fish the river in the manner of a grizzly or Kodiak bear, however they are seen from time to time close to Hudson Bay. Naturally polar bears are revered by all; being the largest North-American predator it is necessary for guides to carry a high-powered rifle during all outings along the Sutton, although they are rarely required to use them.

Recommended services:

(Refer to Appendix B for addresses and phone numbers)

Winisk River Camps

Operated by the Webequie First Nations Indian band, Winisk River Camps offers a number of variable fishing trips on the Winisk River and associated tributaries. Winisk River Camps has a number of guides that are excellent river-men, having spent their entire lives exploring the Winisk area.

Wabusk Expeditions Ltd.

Wabusk Expeditions, operated by Xavier Chookomoolin, is situated on the Sutton River system, and offers fly-in fishing trips on the Sutton River.

Albert's Fishing Camp

Albert's Fishing Camp, also situated on the Sutton River system, is operated by Albert Chokomolin, and specializes in fishing trips on the Sutton River.

Flies and Hatches

RICK NOVAK

JIM SCHOLLMEYER

Nympho (Scott Smith)
Hook: Tiemco 200R/ Daiichi 1270, sizes 8-10
Thread: Orange Uni-Thread 6/0
Tail: Golden pheasant crest
Rib: Gold oval tinsel
Body: Chartreuse Steelhead Dubbin'
Wingcase: 6 strands of peacock hurl
Thorax: Orange or fuschia Steelhead Dubbin'. Pick out fibers to resemble legs
Comments: Tied to the same proportions as a Gold Ribbed Hare's Ear Nymph. Great Lakes steelhead favourite!

Micro Egg (Bob Linsenman)
Hook: Tiemco 3761/Daiichi 1560, sizes 8-10
Thread: Uni-Thread 6/0, red
Body: Two turns orange ultra chenille; four turns silver Mylar tinsel; two turns chartreuse ultra chenille
Comments: Fall steelhead and Chinook salmon fly.

Firefly (Scott Smith)
Hook: Tiemco 3761/Daiichi 1560, sizes 6-10
Thread: Uni-Thread 6/0, black
Body: Chenille (various colours)
Hackle: Filoplume (various colours)
Head: Firefly chartreuse bead head

Cactus Fly (Scott Smith/Mike Sewards)
Hook: Tiemco 105/Daiichi 2571, sizes 4-10
Thread: Uni-Thread 6/0, red
Tail: Tuft of filoplume (various colours)
Body: Several turns of Cactus Chenille (various colours)
Wing: Tuft of filoplume (various colours)
Comments: A must-have steelhead pattern for Superior streams.

Mike's Stone (Scott Smith/Mike Sewards)
Hook: Tiemco 5263, sizes 10-12
Thread: Uni-Thread 6/0, black
Tail: Black goose biots (pair)
Rib: Black balloon strip
Body: Brown dubbing
Wingcase: Turkey quill
Legs: Grouse
Thorax: Ostrich hurl
Antennae: Black goose biots (optional)
Comments: Quill and grouse tied in the "Over the thorax-legs" technique as per Randall Kaufmann's *Fly Tyers Nymph Manual.*

Spring Stone (Scott Smith)
Hook: Tiemco 5263, sizes 4-10
Thread: Uni-Thread 6/0, black
Tail: Red fox squirrel tail
Rib: Gold oval tinsel
Body: Black chenille
Wingcase: Red fox squirrel tail
Thorax: Black chenille
Legs: Brown neck hackle, palmered
Antennae: Red fox squirrel tail
Comments: Good utility stonefly pattern.

Filoplume Hare's Ear (Bill Boote)
Hook: Daiichi 1530, sizes 4-8
Underbody: Lead wire same diameter as hook shank, wrapped full length of shaft
Thread: Danville 6/0, olive
Tail: Grizzly marabou, olive
Rib: Gold oval Mylar size 16/18
Abdomen: Hare's Ear Plus dubbing, olive
Wingcase: Peacock hurl
Thorax: Back shaft of a ring-necked pheasant cock rump feather, palmered forward

BWO/Sulpher Parachute (Barney Jones)
Hook: Daiichi 1130, sizes 14-20
Thread: Griffiths 14/0
Abdomen: Olive/Sulpher quill
Thorax: Olive/black Fine and Dry dubbing
Hackle: Dun/barred ginger hackle
Wing Post: Dun/clear Antron

March Brown Nymph (John Valk)
Hook: Daiichi 1560
Thread: Uni-Thread 8/0, tan
Abdomen: Hare's ear march brown
Thorax: March brown and light brown mixed
Wingcase: Dark turkey quill
Rib: Fine copper wire and black thread wound together

Caddis Larvae Nymph (John Valk)

Hook: Tiemco 2487/Daiichi 1130, sizes 18-22
Thread: Griffiths 14/0, olive
Body: Fine and Dry olive dubbing
Rib: 4-pound-test monofilament (green)
Head: Fine and Dry Adams dubbing

Green Caddis Emerger (John Valk)

Hook: Daiichi 1100/Tiemco 100, sizes 16-20
Thread: Griffiths 14/0, green
Body: CDC under caddis-green hare's ear dubbing
Wing: Natural coloured CDC

Olive Caddis Emerger (Barney Jones)

Hook: Kamasan B-400, sizes 16-20
Thread: Griffiths 14/0, olive
Tail: A few fibres of orange Antron
Body: Fine and Dry olive dubbing
Wing: Coastal deer hair with four strands of pearl Krystal Flash

Blue Belly Dancer (Romeo Rancourt)

Hook: Tiemco 300, size 2
Thread: Uni-Thread 6/0
Tail: Blue marabou with eight strands of royal blue Krystal Flash
Body: Blue Steelhead Dubbin' (lead underbody)
Rib: Fine silver wire
Wing: Chinchilla rabbit strip
Hackle: Red Chinese neck hackle with guinea hackle over top
Comments: Fly should be 4 1/2 inches in length to imitate a Great Lakes smelt. Great flats or river-mouth pattern.

Green-butt Monkey (Scott Smith/Bob Linsenman)

Hook: Tiemco 300/Daiichi 2220, sizes 2-4
Thread: Uni-Thread 6/0
Tail: Chartreuse marabou blood; several strands of gold Krystal Flash
Body: Gold tinsel chenille over a lead underbody
Wing: Rusty brown rabbit strip
Throat: Red yarn
Collar: Pheasant rump
Head: Four to six chunks of cigar-sized tan ram's wool (white ram's wool dyed in black coffee). Wool is tied on tightly, teased with a needle and then trimmed
Comments: Great coaster brook trout/coho salmon pattern.

Zoo Cougar (Kelly Galloup)

Hook: Tiemco 300, sizes 2-4
Thread: Uni-Thread 3/0
Tail: Yellow marabou
Body: Gold or pearl Diamond Braid
Underwing: White calf tail to bend of hook
Wing: Two mallard flank feathers dyed yellowish-tan or yellowish-olive

Head: Sculpin-style head of deer hair clipped wide and flat
Comments: Great all-around trout pattern.

Borger Strip Leech, Nipigon River Style (Bill Boote)

Hook: Daiichi 2220, sizes 2-8
Thread: Uni-Thread 3/0 monocord
Tail: Chartreuse marabou with several strands of Krystal Flash
Rib: Medium French silver wire
Body: Uni-Yarn dark olive Mohair (lead underbody)
Wing: Olive chinchilla rabbit strip
Throat: Red marabou or wool
Hackle: Ring-necked pheasant cock rump feather dyed dark olive
Comments: Length of fly should be roughly double the length of the hook. A standby for the Nipigon River.

Wabigoon Rattler (Scott Smith)

Hook: Mustad 34007, 2/0 or larger
Thread: Uni-Thread 3/0, black
Tail: Chartreuse FisHair 4 inches long with numerous strands of Krystal Flash/Flashabou
Body: Large metallic Mylar tubing covering buck shot rattle lashed to hook
Hackle: Webby, long red hackle
Head: Large silver bead-chain eyes
Comments: Good musky/pike streamer.

Wounded Cheezie (Scott Smith)

Hook: Tiemco 300/Daiichi 2220, sizes 2-4
Thread: Uni-Thread 6/0, orange
Tail: Yellow marabou with several strands of pearl Krystal Flash
Rib: Gold wire
Body: Orange Cactus Chenille (lead underbody)
Wing: Orange rabbit strip
Hackle: Pheasant rump dyed red
Head: Hot orange Sculpin Wool tied in fashion of Green-butt Monkey
Comments: A good pike or fall trout streamer.

Tamblyn Damsel (Romeo Rancourt)

Hook: Tiemco 5212, size 8-10
Thread: Olive or black Uni-Thread 6/0
Tail: Green bucktail mixed with several strands of pine-green Krystal Flash
Wing: Dyed black bucktail or black bear
Body: Six strands of peacock herl
Hackle: Black
Eyes: Black mono (melted) or black plastic bead chain.

Blue Belly Dancer (Romeo Rancourt)

Hook: Tiemco 300 or Daiichi 2220, size 2-4
Thread: Black Uni-Thread 6/0
Tail: Blue marabou with eight strands

of blue Krystal Flash (four on each side)
Rib: Fine silver wire
Body: Steelhead dubbing (blue)
Top: Chinchilla rabbit strip four inches long
Throat: Red webby hackle
Hackle: Natural guinea.

Romeo's Revenge (Romeo Rancourt)

Hook: Tiemco 2457, size 8-10
Weight: Lead or copper wire wrapped in the shape of an egg
Thread: 6/0 Uni-Thread white or beige
Body: Latex balloon with matching Krystal Flash (egg/attractor colours) folded over the egg-shaped lead
Hackle: Remainder of Krystal Flash is pulled back and tied off with a whip-finished head.

Thera Black Stone (Romeo Rancourt)

Hook: Tiemco 9672 size 8-16
Thread: Uni-Thread 6/0 black
Tail: Round rubber hackle black
Body: Thera band material wrap
Thorax: Dark claret (a mix of 50% seal and 50% Hareline Dubbin')
Legs: Grouse feather placed on top of thorax and tied at the eye
Wingcase: Thera band from the body folded on top of the grouse hackle, tied off with a whip-finish.

Thera Golden Stone (Romeo Rancourt)

Hook: Tiemco 9672 or Tiemco 200R, size 8-16
Thread: Yellow Uni-Thread 6/0
Underbody: Medium lead to match hook shank diameter
Tail: Cream round rubber hackle with two spots of brown waterproof marker
Body: Thera band yellow marked on top with brown waterproof marker
Thorax: A mixture of 25% cream seal, 25% brown seal, and 50% gold rabbit dubbings
Legs: Grouse feathers placed on top of thorax and tied at the eye
Wingcase: The remains of thera yellow band is stretched and folded on top of the grouse feather, mark with brown waterproof marker to give mottled look.

The Secret (Romeo Rancourt)

Hook: Mustad 94831 size 12
Tail: Red squirrel tail
Body: Peacock herl twisted and wrapped
Rib: Fine copper wire
Hackle: Brown and grizzly
Head: A small pinch of deer hair approximately the size of a pen tip.

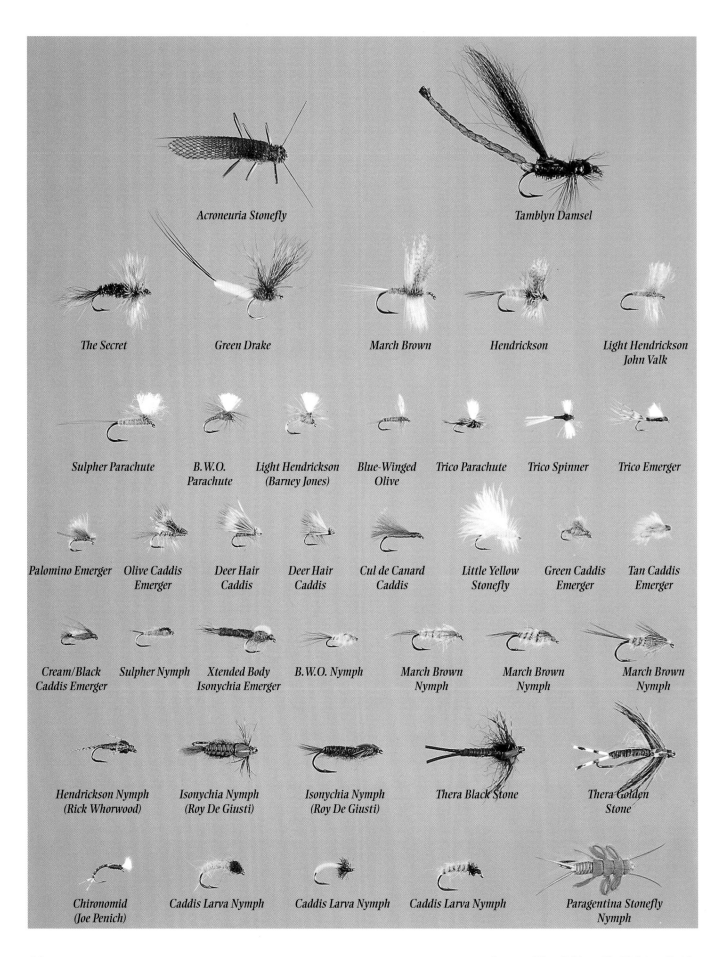

Acroneuria Stonefly

Tamblyn Damsel

The Secret

Green Drake

March Brown

Hendrickson

Light Hendrickson
John Valk

Sulpher Parachute

B.W.O.
Parachute

Light Hendrickson
(Barney Jones)

Blue-Winged
Olive

Trico Parachute

Trico Spinner

Trico Emerger

Palomino Emerger

Olive Caddis
Emerger

Deer Hair
Caddis

Deer Hair
Caddis

Cul de Canard
Caddis

Little Yellow
Stonefly

Green Caddis
Emerger

Tan Caddis
Emerger

Cream/Black
Caddis Emerger

Sulpher Nymph

Xtended Body
Isonychia Emerger

B.W.O. Nymph

March Brown
Nymph

March Brown
Nymph

March Brown
Nymph

Hendrickson Nymph
(Rick Whorwood)

Isonychia Nymph
(Roy De Giusti)

Isonychia Nymph
(Roy De Giusti)

Thera Black Stone

Thera Golden
Stone

Chironomid
(Joe Penich)

Caddis Larva Nymph

Caddis Larva Nymph

Caddis Larva Nymph

Paragentina Stonefly
Nymph

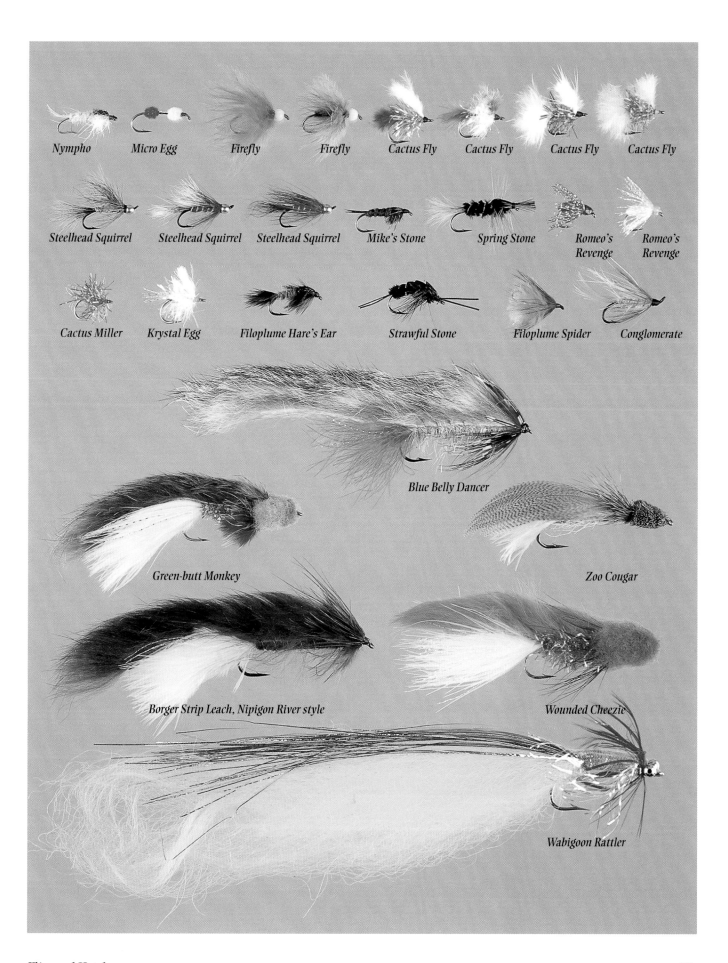

Nympho Micro Egg Firefly Firefly Cactus Fly Cactus Fly Cactus Fly Cactus Fly

Steelhead Squirrel Steelhead Squirrel Steelhead Squirrel Mike's Stone Spring Stone Romeo's Revenge Romeo's Revenge

Cactus Miller Krystal Egg Filoplume Hare's Ear Strawful Stone Filoplume Spider Conglomerate

Blue Belly Dancer

Green-butt Monkey

Zoo Cougar

Borger Strip Leach, Nipigon River style

Wounded Cheezic

Wabigoon Rattler

Northern Ontario Hatch Chart

Compiled by J. Frederick Dean

Common Name	Genus	Hook Size	Hatch Period	Hatch Time
Early Black Stonefly	*Capnia vernalis*	18–22	Mid-March–early May	Midday
Early Brown Stonefly	*Taeniopteryx sp.*	14–16	Early April–mid-May	Midday
Rush Sedge Caddis	*Phryganea cinerea*	6–10	Early April–early July	Midday
Little Tan Short-horn Sedge (caddis)	*Glossosoma intermedium*	12–14	Early April–late August	Afternoon, evening
Early Blue-Winged Olive (mayfly)	*Baetis spp.*	16–18	Early April–late May	Midday
Brown Spinner, Black Quill (mayfly)	*Leptophlebia spp.*	14–18	Early April–late May	Midday
Blue Quill (mayfly)	*Paraleptophlebia spp.*	14–18	Early April–late May	Midday
Hendrickson	*Ephemerella subvaria*	10–14	Early April–late May	Midday
Quill Gordon	*Epeorus pleuralis*	10–14	Early April–late May	Midday
March Brown, Gray Fox (mayfly)	*Stenonema vicarium*	10–12	Early April–late May	Midday
Light Cahill (mayfly)	*Stenacron interpunctatum*	14–18	Mid-April–late June	Midday
Smoky Wing Sedge (caddis)	*Apatania spp.*	14–16	Late April–late May	Midday
Scaly Wing Sedge (caddis)	*Ceraclea spp.*	14–16	Early May–early July	Midday
Salmonfly (stonefly)	*Pteronarcys dorsata*	2–4	Mid-May–early July	Evening
Mahogany Dun (mayfly)	*Isonychia sp.*	10–14	Late May–early July	Afternoon
Spotted Sedge (caddis)	*Hydropsyche slossonae*	14–16	Early June–mid-July	Evening
Dark Blue Sedge (caddis)	*Psilotreta labida*	14–18	Early June–mid-July	Evening
American Grannom (caddis)	*Brachycentrus spp.*	14–16	Early June–mid-July	Evening
Little Black Sedge (caddis)	*Chimarra aterrima*	14–18	Early June–mid-September	Evening
Green Sedge (caddis)	*Rhyacophila sp.*	12–16	Early June–late August	Evening
Little Yellow Stonefly	*Isoperla spp.*	10–12	Early June–late July	Evening
Yellow Sally	*Chloroperla*	12–14	Early June–mid-August	Evening
Eastern Gray Drake (mayfly)	*Siphlonurus quebecensis*	8–10	Early June–early July	Evening
Eastern Golden Stonefly	*Acroneuria evoluta*	8–10	Early June–late July	Afternoon, evening
Great Brown Stonefly	*Acroneuria lycorias*	6–8	Early June–late July	Afternoon, evening
Eastern Creeper (stonefly)	*Perlodidae spp.*	6–8	Early June–late July	Afternoon, evening
Giant Drake (mayfly)	*Hexagenia limbata*	6–8	Late June–early July	Dusk, dark
Brown Drake (mayfly)	*Ephemera simulans*	8–10	Late June–mid-July	Evening, dusk
Great Dive-bomber Sedge (caddis)	*Agrypnia sp.*	8–12	Late June–early September	Evening
White Fly (mayfly)	*Ephoron leukon*	12–14	Late June–late August	Evening
Speckled Spinner (mayfly)	*Callibaetis sp.*	10–14	Late June–late August	Evening
White Miller (caddis)	*Nectopsyche spp.*	8–12	Early August–late Sept.	Evening
Great Orange Sedge (caddis)	*Pycnopsyche spp.*	8–12	Early August–mid-October	Afternoon

Note: sp. - denotes undetermined species   spp. - denotes species plural

Dividing Line Between
Northern and
Southern Hatches

°Ottawa

Southern Ontario Hatch Chart

Compiled by Roy De Giusti & John Valk

Common Name	Genus	Hook Size	Hatch Period	Hatch Time
Early Black Stonefly	*Allocapnia sp.*	16–18	Early April–early May	Midday
Early Blue-Winged Olive (mayfly)	*Baetis spp.*	16–18	Mid-April–mid-May	Midday
Hendrickson (mayfly)	*Ephemerella subvaria*	12–16	Late April–early May	Afternoon
Blue Quill (mayfly)	*Paraleptophlebia spp.*	18–20	Early May–early June	Throughout day
Spotted Sedge (caddis)	*Hydropsyche sp.*	12–14	Early May–late August	Afternoon
Speckled Sedge (caddis)	*Cheumatopsyche sp.*	14–16	Early May–late August	Afternoon
Black Quill (mayfly)	*Leptophlebia spp.*	10	Mid May–early June	Midday
Yellow Stonefly	*Isoperla spp.*	14–16	Mid May–early July	Evening
Gray Fox (mayfly)	*Stenonema fuscum*	10–14	Late May–early June	Afternoon
Pale Evening Dun (mayfly)	*Ephemerella dorothea*	18	Late May–early June	Evening
Little Black Caddis	*Chimarra*	18–20	Late May–early June	Morning
Sulfur Dun (mayfly)	*Ephemerella invaria*	16	Late May–early June	Afternoon, evening
Green Drake (mayfly)	*Ephemera guttulata*	8–10	Late May–early June	Dusk
Brown Drake (mayfly)	*Ephemera simulans*	8–10	Late May–early June	Evening
Giant Drake (mayfly)	*Hexagenia limbata*	4-6	Early June–early July	After dark
Mahogany Dun (mayfly)	*Isonychia sp.*	10	Early June–late September	Evening
Golden Stonefly	*Acroneuria lycorias*			
	Paragentina media	8–10	Early June–mid-July	After dark
Light Cahill (mayfly)	*Stenacron sp.*	14–16	Mid-June–late September	Evening
Salmonfly (stonefly)	*Pteronarcys dorsata*	2–6	Mid-June–late June	After dark
Golden Drake (mayfly)	*Potamanthus sp.*	8–10	Early July–early August	Afternoon
White-Winged Black (mayfly)	*Tricorythodes sp.*	20–22	Early July–late July	Early morning
White Caddis	*Nectopsyche spp.*	12–14	Late July–late September	Dusk
Giant Drake (mayfly)	*Hexagenia atrocaudata*	8	Early August–late September	Throughout day
White Fly (mayfly)	*Ephoron leukon*	14	Mid-August–mid-September	Evening
Blue-Winged Olive (mayfly)	*Pseudocloeon sp.*	22	Late August–mid-September	Throughout day
Great Orange Sedge (caddis)	*Pycnopsyche spp.*	10	Early–late September	Morning

Note: sp. - denotes undetermined species   spp. - denotes species plural

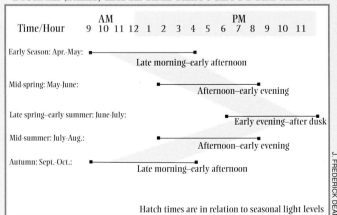

DIURNAL (DAILY) HATCH TIME THROUGHOUT THE SEASON

Hatch times are in relation to seasonal light levels

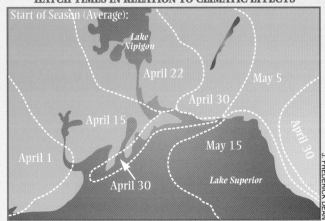

HATCH TIMES IN RELATION TO CLIMATIC EFFECTS

SECTION 3

Inland Frontiers

Inasmuch as Ontario was one of the first settled regions of Canada, her bounty as a fly-fishing destination has just come into its own. For centuries settlers fished for sustenance and, in some cases, visiting dignitaries—mainly from the British Isles—were treated to trophy fishing by government and railway managers. But not until recently has Ontario begun to manage and promote its fishing resources as a tourist attraction. Fly fishing being an environmentally friendly and generally non-consumptive angling sport, it has been included in the provincial thrust for expansion in the eco-tourism market. This thrust brings about many advantageous benefits for the fly angler: stocking programs, harvest reductions, and

Guide Dave Jackson fishes the picturesque West Little White River (Blue Lake System).

stream enhancement projects on the resource management side; and fly shops, guide services and resorts on the business side.

The sport of fly fishing is also making a resurgence of late in a region that several years ago was mainly spin-fishing country. Not that anything is wrong with that discipline, but its strong following reduced fly-fishing circles to cult-like groups, gathering in basements during the winter months to do their "crafts" and secretly talk about tight loops, windknots and other foreign phenomena. Presently, however, fly anglers are either being born or coming out of the closet and making a respectable account of themselves on provincial lakes and streams, fishing for everything that swims.

For these very reasons, I refer to Ontario's inland rivers and lakes as fly-fishing frontiers. Many places have been fished before, but not all with a fly rod.

Northwestern Musky and Pike

The formidable jaws of a northern pike make short work of flies and monofilament leaders.

Few fish—freshwater and saltwater alike—offer the fly angler such excitement and exhilaration as these two cousins: the northern pike and the musky. These are big, toothy, frightening-looking creatures that make short work of monofilament tippets and light-weight rods. Their diet includes ducklings, squirrels and other rodents, and really anything else it cares to eat. Things like whole three-pound walleye, tin cans and pieces of broken outboard propellers have been found in their gullets. This inherent aggressiveness, not to mention its disdain for anything foreign in its territory, make pike and musky fly fishing another irresistible pursuit within the sport. I must confess, being a dyed-in-the-wool trout and steelhead fisherman, that I quickly became addicted to the sheer explosive excitement that goes with pike and musky fishing.

Perhaps the most exciting element of this pursuit comes from the creature's penchant for following its prey. One of my most exhilarating experiences in researching this book came when a "small" twenty-pound musky began following my fly to the boat, lazily poking the tail of the bucktail concoction with its snout. Not just once, but cast after cast for a period of almost thirty minutes this pest would lurch behind my fly, at times even sucking the fly partially into its mouth and then expelling it as it rolled sideways beneath the boat, reminiscent of a scene from Jaws. This continued until my shooting line became so unimaginably tangled at the bottom of the boat (I've since employed the use of a casting apron) that it took me another thirty minutes to unravel. (How a line ties itself in such a composite of knots that you yourself could not create with a crochet needle, remains one of fly fishing's unsolved phenomenon.) During this delay the musky either became tired of the game or found something more worthwhile to chase. In any event, this nasty habit of persistently following artificials makes anglers crazy, in a mesmerizing kind of way. I know it left my knees shaking and I was more determined than ever to hook up with a musky.

Techniques

As I alluded to earlier in this chapter, pike and musky are not regular fare for the fly rod. Their size, aggressiveness, shark-like teeth and unusual diet dictate different techniques. The spring-creek trout enthusiast should take all their tapered leaders, whippy rods, cul-de-canard feathers and knowledge of Latin nomenclature, wrap it up neatly and leave it in their den when they go for big pike and musky. A monofilament tippet—even thirty pound test—will not stand up to musky and pike. Fishing big pike and musky with a fast-action eight-weight rod, nine feet long, is akin to fishing the Restigouche's Atlantics with a six weight. At the minimum, a nine-weight rod would be my recommendation for pike and musky. Personally, I fish a Sage RPLX 1090 rod (saltwater series, ten weight, nine feet). This level of armament is necessary, not only for wrestling big fish out of weed beds, but for casting large wind-resistant flies for long distances on wide-open stretches of water. I prefer a shooting-head line system, which allows for a variety of presentations from surface to about eight feet subsurface; not to mention greater distance casting. In addition, a shooting-head system means that you need only purchase one good reel, and perhaps one extra spool (for those that fish with Abels and let their children go hungry).

The quickest and best leader system I've seen is one that Manitoba pike enthusiast Stu Thompson employs with the use of Mason Nylostrand leader material (a braided-steel leader material with a nylon coating). Stu takes a sixteen- or eighteen-inch length of fifteen-pound Mason Nylostrand and threads one end through the eye of his fly hook. The tag end is left about two inches long, bent sharply back and grasped with a locking hemostat. With the fly held firmly in one hand and the long end of the leader in the other, the hemostat is spun around the main leader numerous times. The result is a tightly twisted leader and fly connection. The other end of the Nylostrand leader is fastened to a fairly short length of monofilament leader with an Albright knot (normally used to fasten backing to fly line). Generally the leader I use is about six feet in total. This includes a twelve- to sixteen-inch length of Nylostrand, and three sections of monofilament stepping up from fifteen- to twenty-five-pound test where it meets the fly line. This leader can be constructed in minutes and is very durable. If you are gunning for musky or very large pike, you may consider stepping up to twenty-pound-test Nylostrand; however this cannot be twisted as easily, and a figure-eight knot must be used to secure the leader to the fly.

Last but not least of the requirements are flies; large and loudly coloured flies. Considering the size of these monsters' standard prey, there is an angling problem to overcome with a fly rod: Inasmuch as you cannot cast a squirrel with a fly rod, neither can you cast a duckling fly either. Subsequently, you must either purchase or construct flies that will

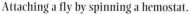

Attaching a fly by spinning a hemostat.

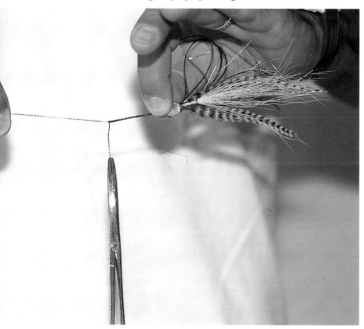

The author double-hauls for musky and pike on Eagle Lake.

attract your adversary, be castable, and at least have the appearance of being fairly big in the water. Many new fly tying materials on the market will enable you to accomplish such a task. Synthetic materials such as FisHair—which resembles bucktail with much less bulk—Krystal Flash and Flashabou (both fluorescent and phosphorescent), and other light reflective materials such as Holographic Fly Fiber, give pike and musky flies flash and colour and enable you to tie them quite long without excessive weight and bulk. The synthetics are also generally more durable than natural materials. Combinations of oranges, reds, whites and yellows should be represented in your fly box, as well as solid black, which stands out well in any water condition. The addition of some type of eye on your fly is important as pike and musky are said to target the head of their prey on the attack. A small rattle incorporated into the fly is also a worthwhile option for any pike or musky pattern.

Tips for casting: Use the double haul religiously; target structure along the bank; and vary your retrieve, which generally should be quite fast. I find that the use of a glove on your rod hand will reduce chaffing and the cutting of your fingers as you strip line. Pike and musky fishing are games of casting; they will definitely hone your casting skills for all other types of fly fishing.

Wabigoon Lake and Eagle Lake

Although musky are represented quite well in most southern areas of the province, and pike virtually everywhere in the province, I have chosen to focus on Northwestern Ontario as the place for pike and musky of monstrous proportions.

Both Wabigoon and Eagle Lake have potential world-record musky in their waters. In fact, Wabigoon Lake, which is situated along the Trans-Canada Highway near the towns of Dryden and Wabigoon, was the site of a biological study on musky in which two muskies exceeding the present world record of approximately seventy pounds were netted and photographed by biologists in the late 1980s. (One musky was conservatively estimated at eighty pounds by one of the project's biologists.) This occurrence, in addition to the fact that I grew up in Dryden fishing the waters of Wabigoon Lake, brought me back to the area to fish in waters that perhaps held the new world-record musky. And I could attain instant fame by catching it on a fly rod!

I fished with high school friend Terry Kluke who now owns and operates Merkel's Fishing Camp on Wabigoon Lake near Wabigoon, Ontario. Terry began his most hospitable guiding foray, that lasted about

A six-inch musky fly is dwarfed by a musky top-water bait.

three days, by showing me the famous photo of the two gargantuan musky over seventy pounds inside a large net on a small aluminum boat. Terry, in fact, assisted in the study, by pointing out to the biologists the haunts of large musky in the area. Terry's knowledge of the lake proved invaluable to the biologists whose study involved capturing, tagging and monitoring the travels and habits of large musky. In addition to the "record" fish that were captured (incidentally they were not tagged due to the fact that the biologists could not physically hang on to them long enough), numerous fish in the forty- to sixty-pound range were netted, fitted with transmitters and monitored over several summers. In addition to the spectacular find of truly enormous musky in the lake, the five-year study showed these large musky had several haunts that they frequented routinely by travelling well-defined routes from bay to bay. As a result of the findings of this study, and from lobbying by lodge owners such as Terry Kluke, the limit on musky was set at one fish per day over 52 inches (two fish in possession). This regulation has greatly benefited the musky population in the lake, as well as the trophy fishing industry in the area. Terry Kluke's paternal commitment to the restoration of the Wabigoon's giant musky and his extensive knowledge of these routes and haunts makes him the ultimate musky guide.

Terry also showed me photographs of a northern pike (about sixteen pounds) that had been mauled by a large musky while being fought by

Abundant hatches of large mayflies establish the base for Wabigoon Lake's bountiful fish population.

one of Terry's guests who was casting from the camp dock. The pike was photographed and released; who knows what fate awaited it in the waters near Merkel's Camp. These photos, and stories about full-grown ducks disappearing from the surface in tremendous boils, add to the folklore of fishing this beautiful area. As we cruised out from Merkel's dock on the first day of musky fishing, I mulled over the accounts that Terry had so eloquently detailed until I finally looked at him and asked, "Do you know where the baby muskies hang out?"

We made several outings over the next three days but failed to click onto a good musky, although we were kept nicely entertained by numerous tenacious pike. We had been plagued by wind and very hot weather. But as Terry points out, "You don't fish for musky, you hunt, and we've only been hunting a few days."

One very interesting technique Terry employs is reminiscent of deep-sea marlin fishing. Terry methodically works one of several large twelve-inch plugs in his box, complete with hula skirts and propellers, on a stout baitcasting outfit, while the client(s) fly cast to likely holding water. He does this to tease the musky—or wake them up, as he puts it—and get them following the plug. Once this occurs the client can deliver a well-placed fly right in front of the cruising musky and hopefully elicit a strike from the fish.

Large musky feed infrequently on large prey, such as three- to five-pound walleye and whitefish; subsequently when these huge fish are not feeding they must be irritated into striking with large, noisy baits and flies incorporating flashy colours, rattles and erratic actions.

Wabigoon Lake is a unique body of water. It is a large, fairly shallow, clay-bottomed lake with inherently murky water; fishing it one hot summer evening I imagined myself fishing in a bayou somewhere.

Cedar Point Lodge at Eagle Lake.

Although non-typical fly-fishing conditions, the richness of this system provides for an abundance of aquatic life. Tremendous hatches of large mayflies, locally referred to and disdained as "fish flies", account ultimately for the existence of trophy musky and pike.

Now before you begin to conjure up thoughts of fishing for musky with a White Wulff, these brutes naturally do not focus on the hatches for sustenance.

What these prolific hatches do for the fishery though, is provide the forage base for large populations of whitefish, lake herrings, walleye, perch and bass that in turn become abundant fare for musky and pike. Whitefish especially are a favoured food of musky and pike. Referencing Schwiebert's *Matching the Hatch,* considering the size and colouration of these "fish flies", and Wabigoon's silt-bottomed waters, the primary hatches are likely *Hexagenia recurvata, Hexagenia limbata* and *Ephemera simulans.*

Wabigoon Lake is maze-like with numerous bays and islands; there are a multitude of shallow coves and bays with thick groves of weeds, providing ideal habitat for musky and pike. On occasion musky can be seen "sunning themselves" on the surface of these weed beds. A good fly caster can plop a fly on the edge, or in a pocket of, a weed bed. Often if there is a pike or musky there they will immediately take the fly.

Given the size of the lake, the numerous islands and bays, and abundance of shallow rock reefs—invisible because of the murky water—fishing without a guide is not recommended.

Naturally I give Terry Kluke the thumbs up as a musky guide. His personal best is a 48-inch musky that he released; in fact no musky have been killed at Merkel's Camp since 1980. The Camp record is a whopping 60-inch fish.

In contrast, Eagle Lake is a body of water that is quite clear, having a more sandy than silt-like bottom. Similarly, however, it is large, maze-like and relatively shallow like Wabigoon. Eagle stretches from just west of Dryden westward well past the town of Vermilion Bay 40 kilometers away. Eagle Lake is serviced by an abundance of fishing resorts that attract mainly walleye, pike and musky anglers from all over Canada and the United States. It is an ideal vacation spot for the family as well, with numerous sandy beaches and pleasant water temperatures during the summer. Once again, it would be unwise to fish Eagle Lake unguided, I chose to fish out of Cedar Point Lodge near Vermillion Bay.

Cedar Point's owner, Pat Hron, is equally committed to the conservation of the area's trophy fishing, as is his colleague and friend Terry Kluke of Merkel's Camp. Cedar Point is a full-scale resort with a large fleet of boats capable of handling up to 100 guests at any given time. I fished with Pat and also one of his top guides, Wayne Lavers. I fished both the north-end of Eagle near the lodge, and a small outpost lake for "small" musky, up to 20 pounds or so. It is here that I experienced the thrill of the "follow-up" by a number of curious musky with apparent lockjaw.

Pat Hron feels that the availability of outpost lakes with an abundance of small muskies and pike, gives the angler a diversity in fishing experiences. Pat can arrange a trip for clients so that they can fish some smaller lakes for "training fish" prior to setting sail on Eagle for the big boys.

Fishing on Eagle Lake, I found that some of the tactics varied slightly with those employed on Wabigoon. Wayne Lavers attributes these differences to the clarity of Eagle's water. Big fish in Eagle Lake tend to dwell in deeper water just off structure like weed beds, referred to by Wayne as "cabbage patches" and sunken islands. Wayne prefers orange-coloured flies and suggests changing your pattern immediately after a follow-up. Evenings are the most productive time of the day—and generally the most pleasant time—for muskies and large pike, which incidentally can be found in the same hangouts. Fishing is productive all season long—late May to October—but a prime time for big musky is prior to freeze-up in October. (Musky season in the Wabigoon-Eagle region is from the third Saturday in June to November 30.) October is also a time when few other anglers are on the lake. Additionally, there is some excellent small-mouth bass fishing (up to five-pound fish) in the fall as well.

Consistent with the conservation philosophy applied to Wabigoon Lake, the legal limit on Eagle Lake for musky is one fish over 48 inches per day and a two-fish possession limit.

These minimum sizes speak volumes to the size of the musky in Wabigoon and Eagle lakes. For the fly angler, landing one of these brutes on a fly rod could be your claim to fame.

There are a number of added bonuses to fishing either of these prolific lakes. The most obvious, other than the existence of record-breaking musky, is the abundance of northern pike. As I mentioned earlier in this chapter, often large pike and musky will inhabit the same haunts. However, as I learned when fishing with both outfitters, there are high-percentage areas for both species.

In areas known for gigantic musky, only the largest of pike will be encountered, for as illustrated in Terry's account of the attack on the sixteen-pound pike, smaller pike become lunch if they frequent these same haunts. There is an abundance of medium-sized pike in both lakes, and a good guide can put you onto dozens of decent pike (between five and fifteen pounds) in one day. Additionally, pike are not pursued with the same vigour as are walleye, which account for the greatest amount of tourist fishing in Northwestern Ontario. Subsequently, you can find yourself fishing some very productive pike water with little competition.

Although there seems to be a little more pressure on musky haunts, these areas are generally fished by a boat for an hour at a time on a rotating basis. Flogging the same stretch of water for hours on end is not a productive musky tactic.

The dogs days of summer during July and August, when fly fishing on most trout streams in Ontario is generally poor, are prime time for top-water angling for large pike and musky. October is also prime-time, but generally flies must be presented deep as these predators lurk near rocky points and reefs to feed on walleye and whitefish that congregate near drop-offs and transition points.

Autumn is a high-percentage time for musky on Wabigoon Lake.

Quetico Bass

A Quetico smallmouth bass.

S mallmouth bass are becoming more and more synonymous with the sport of fly fishing as fly anglers turn on to this species' reputation as a fighter, jumper, and lover of surface flies.

Similar to northern pike, smallmouth are widely distributed throughout the Province—especially along the entire U.S. border, below the 49th parallel. Like any type of angling, the fishing gets progressively better the farther you trek into the wilderness. It is for this very reason that Quetico Park's bass fishing has received due attention in several fly-fishing publications. It is renowned for large and abundant smallmouth bass in a truly wilderness setting.

Quetico Provincial Park is a wilderness park situated just outside Superior's watershed, which ends some 40 miles west of the Ontario port city of Thunder Bay. Access is limited to non-motorized craft, mainly canoes and kayaks. The park's waterways, formed by the scouring glaciers of the Ice Age some nine-thousand years ago, eventually make their way to the Arctic Ocean in round-about fashion through Lake Winnipeg in Manitoba. Many of Quetico's elongated lakes are brimmed by spectacular cliffs and boulder deposits, making ideal canoe routes and giving the paddling visitor a welcomed reprieve from rough weather. Most importantly though, this same condition—narrow, river-like lakes chiseled from formations of glacial rock—makes Quetico's lakes a trophy destination for smallmouth bass.

Anglers visiting the 2800-square-mile park must enter at one of a select number of access points on a prearranged basis. The popularity of Quetico has necessitated park managers to set a limit on the amount of human activity at any given time within the park to preserve its61
 wilderness essence. Only one road, the Dawson Road Trail, exists within the park. All other travellers must use non-motorized craft for transportation.

Appropriately, canned and bottled goods are not allowed within the interior of the park. All food containers must be burned or packed out. Considering the long and grueling portages that link lakes and rivers together and form an integral part of any canoe route, the ban on canned and bottled goods is a veritable blessing. The wise angler economizes carefully so that portages can be made in one trip, without having to leave packs behind while returning for more. Black bears can be a nuisance in well-travelled areas and an abandoned food pack is too much of a temptation for these four-legged brigands.

Fraught with history, Quetico's 900 miles of canoe routes were first developed by the French regime in the early 1700s to establish fur-trading routes and trading posts. After their defeat in 1759 the French relinquished these posts to the British who further developed routes from both Grand Portage (Minnesota) and Fort William (Ontario) connecting Superior with points west and ultimately the Pacific Ocean. The Northwest Company (now the Bay Company) developed the renowned Dawson Route (portions of which can still be travelled today) to move their furs by both road and waterway in the late 1800s. The parks aboriginal roots are evident in numerous Indian pictographs and century-old artifacts. These may be photographed but not touched.

Over the years I have trekked in Quetico a number of times, and consistent with the experience of most, each time I venture farther into the park and stay for longer periods. In itself, this type of wilderness vacation is a subculture. It requires specialized gear, confidence and ingenuity in equipment, and considerable knowledge in wilderness skills, such as compass and map work.

When you are carrying all your gear in the canoe—and more importantly on your back through grueling portages—you must be wise in your selection of fly-fishing equipment. I suggest you use a good-quality pack rod in a seven- or eight-weight. A spare rod is probably a good idea too, if you can find a place to put it. Carry a good, dependable reel loaded with floating line (bass tapers are nice), and a spare spool with

A lightning strike in Quetico Park.
Following page: The author prepares for some early morning dry-fly fishing in Quetico Park. Rick Novak photo.

either a shooting system or a fast-sinking sink-tip. Flies should include an array of standard streamers (I favour rabbit-strip patterns because of their action), poppers and patterns such as the Dahlberg Diver. You'll also need a good collection of larger dries, such as Wulffs, Stimulators and other *Hexagenia* and stonefly imitations.

While researching this book during the summer of 1996, I encountered the most incredible hatch of stoneflies (great brown stoneflies, *Acroneuria lycorias*) that I have ever seen, near the outlet of a small lake. My good friend and professional photographer, Rick Novak, carefully maneuvered the canoe in the current just above a thundering set of waterfalls, as I casted a Yellow Stimulator to a number of huge smallmouth that chose this precarious feeding station. I managed to hook and land a smaller fish—about three pounds—but the biggest fish continually refused my Stimulator. I can only attribute this to the possibility that the hatch was so prolific that the fish could afford to be quite selective in their tastes. And why not? There were so many stoneflies coming off the water that they were crawling up our paddles and gathering in the bottom of our canoe.

Good mayfly hatches are also encountered in the park. During this same trip I noticed some decent rises just outside our island campsite one morning after coffee. On closer inspection I noticed a considerable number of light-coloured spinners on the water, and after a bit of trial-and-error fly changing, I hooked and landed my very first walleye on a dry fly. (I might add that this decent two-pounder became lunch, and I quote from John Gierach now, "In every fly fisherman's past there is a black frying pan.")

Getting away from the finer arts and back to reality, it is highly recommended that you stow away a length of Mason Nylostrand in your vest as pike are also very abundant in Quetico.

Although there are exceptions to every rule, the best bass fishing in Quetico seems to be in areas of current. There are many lakes in the park that are narrow and have river-like currents. The bass are often concentrated in these areas, with the biggest bass in the prime lies behind rocks and in the eye of the pool. There are places where you can wade and fish current tongues and pools from rock outcroppings. I encountered a great session of afternoon fishing by casting a sinking head out into a pool and letting the strong current sweep my streamer through the pool as I stood on a rock shelf. The bass would follow the big streamer like a trout and ambush it on the swing. Great fun.

A productive technique for fishing from a canoe, especially fishing new, unexplored water, is to have the bow angler cast to likely holding lies along the shoreline, while the stern angler trolls a fly and paddles about 50 feet from shore. This way you can explore the shoreline and look for prime smallmouth haunts at the same time. Once you hook-up, or locate some likely looking cover, you can stop the canoe and work it thoroughly.

The best way to incorporate fishing time into your travel schedule is to fish in the early morning and evening hours, leaving the unproductive midday period for covering large distances on the water. Keep in mind though, that if wind conditions are tough, you may have to reverse this pattern in the interest of safety and economy of efforts.

Considering all the trips I have done in the park, the most enjoyable trip is a circle route, which means you never see the same water twice. When planning a circle route, make sure you add a little time into your plans for fishing delays. Conversely, don't let the overall length of some routes discourage you; it is surprisingly easy to cover 15 kilometers of water in one day—even if you take your time and smell the trilliums (Ontario's official flower) along the way.

There are numerous routes one can take depending on how deep and how long you intend to venture into the interior; similarly there are far too many good bass lakes in the park to mention. In keeping with the notion of "less pressure/better fishing," the interior, less-travelled, portion of the park offers better fishing. Several outfitters cater to canoeists by providing all the necessary gear, including maps and drop-off services. Access to certain areas is limited; subsequently your travel itinerary should be booked well in advance of your trip. Late May is often good timing for bass fishing; not to mention being a slower time of the year for bookings. (Booking information for Quetico Park can be obtained by calling 807 597-2735.)

CHAPTER 8

North of Superior

A north-of-Superior brook trout in full spawning colours.

While reading this chapter, my deep passion and love for this area of the world will no doubt become obvious. This is where I learned to fly fish; my roots and desires for this wonderful sport were born among the spirited wilderness streams of this region, known affectionately as North of Superior.

Over and above the many pristine nursery tributaries of Superior that line its entire shore from Thunder Bay to Sault Ste. Marie, are many inland lakes and streams that are teaming with resident brook trout.

The boundary of this huge catchment area goes from the western limit of Superior's watershed 40 kilometers west of Thunder Bay, to a point near Sault Ste. Marie where the streams east of that city begin to flow towards Lake Huron. The northern limit of this catchment varies from a few kilometers in the most rocky regions to almost 100 kilometers in other areas. Happily, virtually every waterway that ultimately terminates in Superior is home to brook trout; the heritage "trout" species of this wilderness area of Ontario. Most creeks, streams and rivers are either presently inhabited by brookies or were at one time or another. Brook trout (actually a char *Salvelinus fontinalis*) are a species of cold, clean water. In many ways they are an environmental indicator of sorts: The aquatic version of the coal miner's canary, their absence in former ranges is indicative of a decline in water conditions. Conditions that may have degenerated due to toxic effluent or, more simply, careless logging practices that have increased sediment levels—making successful spawning impossible. Fortunately many streams are still relatively unspoiled by such atrocities and still abound with brook trout.

In contrast to the relatively infertile nursery streams of Superior's coast, there are many smaller creeks and streams within the headwater systems of large rivers, such as the Black Sturgeon, the Nipigon and the Goulais, that are prolific mesotrophic or eutrophic waters, capable of sustaining substantial populations of fish. In fact, there are a number of true spring creeks in this region.

Additionally, there is an abundance of clean, productive lakes in the hilly and mountainous regions north of Superior. Most have either natural or stocked populations of brook trout; some are home to giants up to and exceeding the eight-pound mark.

In the interest of brevity, and fairness to the merits of other regions of the province, I will not delve deeply into the names and locations of these lakes. Rather, I suggest interested anglers access readily available Ministry of Natural Resources maps, which indicate both stocked and natural lakes for brook trout, or contact a guide service mentioned in this book.

On a positive conservation note, many lakes with natural populations of trophy brook trout have been closed to winter (ice) fishing; a season when brook trout are exceptionally vulnerable to harvest. Additionally, the harvest of larger fish year-round has been curtailed recently by the reduction of the daily bag limit of five, to a slot limit of five fish with only one fish exceeding 12 inches in length. Hopefully this conservation trend will continue; especially on lakes and streams renowned for bigger brook trout, where an even more conservative bag limit would be very beneficial.

Arrow River

The Arrow River is a medium-sized stream situated at the west end of Superior's drainage, south of the village of Kakabeka Falls on the Trans-Canada Highway. The Arrow is a tributary of the Pigeon River, which forms the border between Ontario and Minnesota before it flows into Superior. The Arrow does not receive any migratory runs of fish due to a series of insurmountable falls on the Pigeon.

In several ways the Arrow River is a non-typical stream in the Superior watershed. It is a clear-water, freestone mesotrophic stream, with both gravel and sand bottom, and a very fishable riffle-run-pool make-up. It also differs in that it does not support a natural population of brook trout, due to the higher than appropriate temperature regimes found in the Arrow.

The most significant and delectable difference is that the Arrow has a considerable self-sustaining population of brown trout thanks to the membership of the Thunder Bay Fly Fishing Club, who subjected the Arrow to a substantial brown trout stocking program between 1990 and 1995. During those years the club stocked a large number of brown trout (fry, fingerling and adult fish) from both riverine and anadromous stocks. In the past few years respectable numbers of large adult fish—some in excess of twenty inches—have been observed on spawning beds. (Successful spawning is evident in the presence of young-of-the-year fish.)

In many ways the river is reminiscent of famed Michigan streams, such as the Pere Marquette and the Little Manistee, with exception of the existence of more rock structure. The river has many prolific hatches, including brown trout mainstays such as the *Hexagenia limbata* and the *Acroneuria evoluta* (golden stonefly). Although this fishery is brand new, its uniqueness makes it definitely worthy of mention. It is difficult to fish, or, at least difficult for us local brook trout anglers to master. Perhaps the key here will be learning how to properly fish for brown trout.

By far the most learned student of the Arrow is Thunder Bay Fly Fishing Club faithful, Frederick Dean. Fred is in essence the father of the Arrow River project and through this he has come to understand the river in a true paternal sense. He has mapped and named many of the pools; cataloged its hatches; caught, released and photographed many of its large denizens.

Speaking of catch-and-release, the entire river is covered by a no-kill regulation. This is further broken down into a 12-kilometer section of fly-fishing-only water (one of a few in Ontario), and the remainder subject to a single-hook-barbless/no-organic-bait regulation. The fly-fishing-only section starts from below the Arrow Lake dam (the source of the river), to the Hartington/Robbins Township line. Although the dam is of the top-draw variety, for most of the year it moderates and cools the temperature of the river in this top section. It is a beautiful stream to fish.

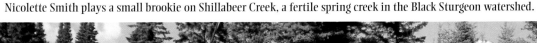

Nicolette Smith plays a small brookie on Shillabeer Creek, a fertile spring creek in the Black Sturgeon watershed.

Shillabeer Creek, a virtual brook trout factory.

Highly wadible (although crossings are made at times quite precariously), with numerous under cut banks, sweepers and flotsam to provide cover; gravel bottomed riffles and tailouts to fish during hatches; and deep bend pools to provide refuge for those wily old browns that are the subject of every fly angler's dreams.

Because of its inherent clear water conditions, the Arrow is best fished during early mornings and evenings. My favourite outing to this home water is an after-work affair: leaving the office at 4:00 or 5:00 p.m., catching the Big Mac hatch on the way out of the city and fishing from 6:00 p.m. right into dark. During the Hex hatch, or what Michigan writer and friend Bob Linsenman affectionately refers to as *Hexaritaville*, it is naturally best fished well into the night. It is at this bright-stars-and-shiny-moon juncture that the still night is erupted by the toilet-flush-like rises of the Arrow's biggest browns.

In early July of 1998, Bob Linsenman made a trip to Thunder Bay to put on a seminar for the Thunder Bay Fly Fishing Club on how to fish the Hex hatch. Preceded by an afternoon slide-show, Bob joined a group of us on the Arrow to fish the Hex hatch into the night. We were delighted to see Bob land two huge browns on *Hexagenia* dun patterns sometime after midnight with Fred as his guide. One fish was estimated at five pounds and the second a whopping eight. This was certainly proof enough for us that the brown-trout project was a worthwhile effort.

Except at night, I fish the Arrow with my lovely Sage 4-weight, light line, nine-footer. In my experience the Arrow seems "Stimulator water. " At least that is the dry fly I carry and fish most on the river. There is a good stonefly representation here, and the fuzzy, floatable Stimulator pattern stays high and dry in the many choppy riffles and runs on the Arrow. Additionally the same pattern makes a good hopper imitation. In the daytime there is an abundance of runs that can be carefully prospected with a good nymph, such as the ubiquitous G.R. Hare's Ear nymph, or a number of other equally standard and productive patterns. At certain times a Muddler will entice bigger fish in large pools, as will a rabbit-strip leech pattern.

At this point I apologetically digress to a time in my personal fly-fishing evolution where rivers were defined by the fly that produced best in their waters. Hence rivers were denoted by my backwoods colleagues and me as either "Woolly Bugger" or "Muddler" rivers, as such was the extent of our repertoire of flies and wisdom.

In keeping with this private idiosyncrasy, after much scrutiny and careful research, we have blithely determined that the Arrow is both a "Woolly Bugger" and a "Muddler" river!

Open season for brown trout on the Arrow is from the last Saturday in April to September 15.

Shillabeer Creek

Shillabeer Creek is one of those true spring creeks I spoke of in the introduction to this chapter. Water-quality studies of this placid, meandering creek are comparable to the mineral make-up of famous Western spring creeks, such as Nelson's and Armstrong's spring creeks. The Shillabeer is a tributary of the Black Sturgeon River, which ultimately empties into Black Bay on Superior, about 80 kilometers east of Thunder Bay. The Shillabeer's origin is a series of groundwater springs near Shillabeer Lake and Fog Lake, which converge into a lowland creek that averages thirty feet in width and five or six feet in depth. The thick weed growth in the creek appears like giant moss outcroppings that often brush the bottom of your canoe as you paddle along and fish the deep, sandy bend pools and weedbed channels. The creek's only inhabitants are native brook trout. No migratory species reach the Shillabeer due to dams on the Black Sturgeon. The brookies of the Shillabeer are prolific in numbers, with most of the catch—which typically is twenty or more fish per angler a day—around the ten-inch mark. However, there are several larger fish to be had in the twelve- to sixteen-inch category. Some of my friends talk of three- and four- pound fish from this creek in past years, and although I cannot personally attest to such glory, I have seen fish take flies off the water in turbulent splashes that I thought only beavers made.

This is a prime example of a stream that has benefited from slot limits, and would most definitely make the trophy-hunt list if special regulations were placed on it.

In reference to my digression in the Arrow River section of this chapter, the Shillabeer is most definitely a "Muddler River". Indeed the best way to fish this sweet little creek is with a Muddler Minnow. To be more precise, a small size 10 or 8 Muddler fished from a canoe on a four-weight with a short durable leader of about six feet long. Short leaders are the ticket for rapidly punching out repetitive casts to small pockets and undercut banks with little back-cast room. My good friend (and local brook trout guru), Bruce Miller, and I fish the creek in turn. One paddles while the other sits in the bow and fires a Muddler to within inches of the bank and then begins a pulsating retrieve. The length of the cast is adjusted so this action can be done by twitching the rod up and back alone, without stripping—which ultimately leads to lost time and tangles. Obviously you must fish water before the canoe traverses, and a good navigator at the stern will keep the canoe on the shallow side of the numerous bends on the Shillabeer. Any stick, log or chunk of weed on the bottom will host a brookie or two. Sometimes surprisingly big brookies will appear from the smallest of cover. Big brookies in such environs are wily. You must pull the trigger quick on the take, keep your line tight and tip high to hold the brookie out of the tangles. You will never get a second chance on the same day with the same fish if they are big: At least according to Bruce.

Frazer River

Another gem is the Frazer River. Very similar to the Arrow River in appearance and character, the Frazer flows from Elizabeth Lake south to its confluence with the mighty Nipigon River. Anything connected to the Nipigon has potential for brook trout, and the Frazer is no exception. For the most part its brookies are "brookies". A name which to me means relatively small and spunky. But similar to the Shillabeer, the Frazer does have the odd big old brook trout that exceeds the sixteen-inch mark.

The Frazer can be picked up off Elizabeth Lake Road, which bears to the west just north of Cameron Falls Dam on Highway 585 along the Nipigon River. The river at this point is churning pocketwater, with numerous falls and rapids, intermingled with placid deep runs bearing ample weed growth. A section of the river north of these rapids meanders for several kilometers and can be fished nicely from a canoe. This meandering stretch of sandy-bottomed, clear-water river culminates at a lake-like pool. Good fishing is available here, but unless there is a decent hatch on you must get down towards the bottom with a good-sized streamer. Above this large pool is a stretch of some of the most formidable pocket water and boreal jungle-lined river bank known to man. I once dropped a brand new Fenwick rod/Hardy reel combination into the drink while attempting to liberate my Muddler (the Frazer being a "Muddler/Woolly Bugger river") from an overhanging cedar. The brisk current quickly stole my rod and reel and swept it downstream while I stood dumbfounded hanging onto the fly line. In a New York minute the reel was spooled of line and backing, but fortunately this climactic turning point coincided with the Fenwick running aground on some flotsam. I ran downstream like a banshee—much to the puzzlement of Bruce who hadn't the foggiest idea what I was doing—and ultimately recovered my entire outfit unscathed, save for a couple of substantial scratches on my virgin Golden Prince reel.

This section of treacherous water is naturally where the best brook trout hang out. The pocket water is interspersed with small runs and another large pool at the base of an old log chute.

This little river that averages thirty feet in width fishes nicely all through the summer, with the pocket-water stretch fishing very good during the heat of summer when oxygen and temperature levels in more moderate flows become poor.

Pukaskwa River

Just east of the town of Marathon on Superior's north shore is Pukaskwa National Park (pronounced Puck-a-saw). This is a region along the shore that was too rugged for both the builders of the railway and the Trans-Canada Highway to traverse. Instead they pushed these thoroughfares north to bypass this area typified by mountainous and craggy terrain, inadvertently sectioning off what is still a very wild, remote and virtually uninhabited area along Superior's northern coast. Through this no-man's land travels the dark and mysterious Pukaskwa River. Because of these same conditions, the Pukaskwa is rarely fished, and subsequently is home to some fabulous fishing. Above the barrier to steelhead and other migratory fish are miles upon miles of untamed river. Catching brook trout in this area is simple. Cast, retrieve, set. That is all there is to it. Some of these brook trout are decent sized, and even trophy sized—over eighteen inches. The true calling of this pretty river however is its majesty in beauty and remoteness. Only a few outfitters have the wherewithal to manage trips on the Pukaskwa. One such outfitter is Bill Day of Superior Ecoventures. Bill flies his clients to the headwaters of the Puk and paddles for seven full days to Hatties Cove, where upon arrangement a charter boat picks up the party and sails back to Marathon.

Canoeing the Pukaskwa is not for beginners. Even the journeyman canoeist would be wise to use a guide that knows the river and keeps up with current water conditions and levels. June (just after spring runoff) is generally the best time of year to fish the Pukaskwa River.

In addition to the Pukaskwa there are a number of rivers and lakes in Pukaskwa National Park that are worth exploring.

East Goulais River

The East Goulais River is a fly-fishing-only branch of the larger Goulais River. This branch begins above the Whittman Dam near Searchmont, and was the site of another planting of brown trout in the early 1990s. Eric Eppert, owner of Fish Tales Custom Tackle in Sault Ste. Marie, fishes this scenic area for browns, rainbows and brookies. The river is easily wadible and has a nice combination of riffles, pools and pocket water to fish for trout that are typically small, up to thirteen or fourteen inches. Smaller mayflies are matched quite nicely with varying sizes of the Blue-Winged Olive on the East Goulais.

Upper Chippewa River

The scenic Chippewa River is best known for its steelhead and salmon fishery near the Trans-Canada Highway. A roadside rest stop has been constructed at this site and a plaque signifies the Chippewa River Bridge as being the center point in Canada for the Trans-Canada Highway. From this vantage point you will notice a churning set of falls that generally create the end of the line for migratory salmonids. However, under ideal conditions steelhead have conquered the falls and over the years a river-ine population of rainbow trout has naturalized in the countless miles of freestone river from above the falls to its headwaters. These stretches are remote but can be accessed through backroad accesses. Typically this headwater portion of the Chippewa is easily wadible, hosting good numbers of resident rainbow trout. Eric Eppert of Fish Tales Custom Tackle in Sault Ste. Marie reports good hatches of stoneflies and caddis from these tea-stained headwaters of the upper Chippewa.

Recommended Services:

(Refer to Appendix B for addresses and phone numbers.)

River's Edge Fly Shop
Superior Fly Fishing
Superior Ecoventures
Bill Day operates Superior Ecoventures and specializes in canoe and kayak trips along the north shore of Superior, including some trips on Lake Superior. Bill is a very experienced woodsman with superior boat handling skills. He also teaches associated courses at Lakehead University in Thunder Bay.

Fish Tales Custom Tackle
Karl Vogel

Nipigon's Giant Brook Trout

The secnic Nipigon River.

In Chapter 1, I covered the lower stretch of the Nipigon River, where good populations of both resident and anadromous brook trout are encountered, along with some dynamite fishing for both summer steelhead and resident rainbow trout. In this chapter, I will cover the top three sections of the Nipigon River where the biggest and baddest brook trout anywhere in the world are known to thrive.

The brook trout of the Nipigon are large, unusually thick-shouldered fish, on account of the richly productive waters of the system. A system that at one time was an untethered river is now a tailwater fishery created by three dams that were constructed during the first half of the twentieth century. This harnessing of the river has obviously changed and tamed the river. If you were old enough to fish the river before and after the damming, you would hardly recognize it, save for the clear, clean flows that are the hallmark of the Nipigon.

Although this harnessing of the river has changed its nature dramatically, there are inherent benefits with any tailwater fishery. What was lost in brisk flows and thundering rapids is gained in the intrinsic aquatic life brought about by the productivity of dammed water. In addition, the reaches of river above the dams are left untainted by the introduction of exotic species to Lake Superior. There are no steelhead and salmon anywhere above Alexander's Dam to compete with the natural populations of brook trout, lake trout and whitefish.

Considering the significance the Nipigon River has played in the angling history of Ontario, a succinct history lesson is in order. The Nipigon was first fished by settlers (mainly British and European) in the late eighteen-hundreds. By the early nineteen-hundreds, the river's reputation for exceptionally large and relatively easily caught brook trout was beginning to circulate. Dignitaries and royalty from around the world were being entertained on the Nipigon by the executives of the Canadian National Railway, which at that time terminated at the Nipigon River. The railway's "sportsman's representative" Neil McDougall guided the likes of Prince Arthur and the Duke of Windsor after reports of huge brook trout had reached the angling elite in England. Photo records of their catches are astounding: dozens of chunky brook trout all between five and ten pounds hung from birch poles. Indeed a few years earlier in 1915, a physician from Port Arthur (now Thunder Bay), Dr. J. W. Cook, landed a whopping fourteen-and-a-half-pound brook trout after a grueling battle on the upper river near the outlet of Lake Nipigon.

As recorded in Edwin Mills' book *Paddle Pack and Speckled Trout,* the Cook fish was taken on July 21, 1915, at approximately 6:00 p.m. Dr. Cook was fishing with three other companions at Rabbit Rapids on the Upper Nipigon. He reportedly skewered a live sculpin minnow—known as a cockatouche—onto his hook, even though a heavy hatch of "brown flies" covered the water's surface. Initially the trout—which took an exhausting period to land on a five-ounce rod—was believed to have been a mackinaw (or lake trout) by Cook and his friends; but after their group of guides and cooks began to chatter incessantly in Ojibwa about the enormous "Hansenmagos" (Ojibwa for brook trout) the naive white-men came to the realization that this was the grand-daddy of all Nipigon brookies. Wisely, Cook had the fish examined by ichthyological authorities in Washington, Ottawa and Toronto. Indeed it was identified as *Salvelinus fontinalis;* all 31 1/2 inches of it. Today the whereabouts of the last existing half of the giant's skin is unknown. Only a graphite replica of the fish rests on a wall in the Ministry of Natural Resources office in Nipigon, Ontario—reminiscent of a colourfully adorned steelhead.

Throughout the majority of the twentieth century, the Nipigon's brook trout have endured many obstacles. Naturally the reports of its enormous brook trout brought angling pressure from everywhere. And naturally, prior to the conceptual beginnings of catch and release in the last twenty years, most, if not all, of her brook trout were harvested, and even fed to dogs, as some reports indicate. This factor, combined with the ever fluctuating levels of water dictated by hydroelectric demands, brought the population of Nipigon's brook trout into a precarious state. Fortunately, due in part to the conservation efforts and lobbying by angling groups and committed biologists, such as the Thunder Bay Fly Fishing Club and Rob Swainson of Nipigon MNR, big and abundant brook trout are making a comeback on the river.

There are a couple of significant factors in this recovery. One major contributor to the increase in brook trout population is an agreement with Ontario Hydro on water levels that has created a more constant flow on the river, and more importantly, a limit on the minimum flow during the spawn. The second factor, and a key factor in my estimation, is the reduction in the legal harvest of brook trout. Only a few years ago, one angler could harvest five brook trout of any size from the Nipigon. Subsequently, a knowledgeable angler could legally, and quite regularly, harvest in excess of twenty pounds of brook trout in one day. In the last decade the daily bag limit has been changed; first to a limit of two fish per day of a minimum length of eighteen inches, and finally to a one-fish limit of a minimum size of twenty inches. Many anglers, including myself, have noted a marked increase in the mean size of fish on the Nipigon since the change in harvest regulations was first introduced. Gradually more fish of trophy stature (over eighteen to twenty inches) have become commonplace. Many anglers, myself included, would like to see an even bigger minimum size—say twenty-four inches—to really augment the river's trophy potential. Perhaps another world record could become reality. In the past several years fly anglers have released fish in excess of eight pounds every year. Those are indeed giant brook trout!

As unique as this mighty river is, with its high canyon walls and aqua-coloured depths, so are the techniques employed here. Many anglers consider the Nipigon a hardware river, feeling that it is generally not suitable for fly angling. I could not disagree more with this decree. What the river dictates is a departure from standard fly-fishing techniques. Techniques that a select number of successful fly anglers, including myself, have developed over the years to conquer this big, brawling, deep river.

The best way to understand this type of river and her fish, is to read up on the nature of fly-fishing rivers. One of the best books on "how to read rivers" is Dave Hughes', *Reading the Water* (Stackpole Books). In this easy-reading book, Dave articulates the common situations and river types that one will encounter anywhere you fish.

As I mentioned in Chapter 1, the fish of the Nipigon are primarily bank-dwellers. The reasons for this are nicely articulated in Dave's book. The Nipigon is a tailwater fishery, which tends to create stable flows near the bank, and it is a deep, fast river, with an abundance of rip-rap and other structure along the bank. As *Reading the Water* points out, rivers such as these provide all the necessary needs of a trout—shelter from current, protection from predators, amiable temperature and oxygen regimes, and the availability of food—along the bank. Hence your angling efforts need to be channeled appropriately.

Bryan Broderick releases a healthy brook trout on the Nipigon River, where lower limits and size restrictions have improved both the numbers and the size of fish.

Ken High (owner of Dr. Slick Fly Tying Tools) with an eight-pound lake trout taken on a large streamer in the Nipigon River.

The most effective way to fish the three upper stretches of the Nipigon River are from a small boat or square stern canoe. One would naturally assume that since the fish in the river are bank-dwellers, as I've just informed, that walk-and-wade tactics would suffice. The problem is, there are very few places to wade and the high canyon walls of the Nipigon make it almost impossible to walk along the bank in places, never mind execute a back cast. Subsequently, the technique that provides the most mobility and ease of angling is to fish from a small boat either anchored or held by the motor in the current. Fly fishing from a boat held stationary in the current by a sputtering outboard may seem sacrilegious to some but anchoring a boat successfully and safely in twenty feet of swiftly flowing river is a guide's nightmare. I'll put up with the motor and save on the perils of fooling with anchors and ropes in death-defying waters.

One of the best ways to fish the shoreline on the Nipigon is a technique developed by River's Edge Fly Shop owner Bill Boote. Bill holds the boat in the current with the motor, so that the boat holds stationary or gradually drifts downstream. Casts are made from a bow casting-platform towards the bank; almost right to the bank in fact. Generally this brand of fishing is of the streamer variety with a sink-tip or shooting head. The fly is allowed to sink by employing a reach cast and large mends immediately after the completion of the cast. Once the fly reaches the appropriate depth, action is imparted to the streamer as it completes the swing through a prime lie, such as a current seam or behind a rock. When fishing this system, takes are signified by the unmistakable jolt of the fly rod that starts at the fly and rolls up the fly line like the whip of a garden hose. Brook trout are rarely subtle when taking a streamer. Newcomers to this type of fishing often have trouble managing sink-tip lines, but after a little practice, casts from fifty to seventy-five feet become routine. After years of boat fishing, Bill and I are quite adept at flinging the entire fly line. Indeed the ability to cast great distances are of primary importance anywhere on the Nipigon River.

A typical day of fishing on the big river involves fishing from the boat with streamers on sink-tip lines throughout the day, followed by an evening walk-and-wade sojourn on a gravel flat during the often prolific hatch that precedes nightfall. Fishing from the boat during a hatch seems to put the fish down, perhaps because of the disturbances the boat makes near the surface.

The upper reaches of the Nipigon River are defined by the three concrete dams on the river: Alexander's, Cameron Falls and Pine Portage.

As you travel north on Highway 585 from the town of Nipigon on the Trans-Canada Highway, the first dam you encounter will be Alexander's. Below this dam is the best stretch of walk-and-wade water on the entire river (covered in Chapter 1). Immediately above Alexander's is a lake-like widening of the river; this is where the Frazer River empties into the Nipigon. Good fishing, both streamer and dry, is available in this lake area along the rocky shore. Above this lake portion and immediately below Cameron Falls Dam is a swift section of river. This is generally fished from shore, by hopping from one rock to another and fishing downstream from your position.

Above Cameron Falls Dam is another lake-like widening of the river known as Jessie Lake. Jessie is renowned for both lake trout and brook trout fishing. The latter of which are concentrated around the islands and sunken reefs in the middle of the lake. Incidentally, it is here on Jessie Lake that while loading my boat onto the trailer one July evening after a full day of fishing on the river, that I encountered an incredible spinner fall of huge *Hexagenia limbata*. My fishing companion Bruce Miller and I, quickly stowed all our heavy gauge streamer equipment and waded into the lake at dusk with a floating six-weight and some large dries. We were soon surrounded by large swirls made by voraciously feeding brookies and whitefish. We failed to capitalize on this feast due in part to the incredible hatch of mosquitoes that were in turn feeding voraciously on us. In addition, we were attempting to fish our normal twelve-foot dry-fly leaders that sure enough, spent most of the fishing time wrapped around one thing or another. I have since learned that in order to fish the hex spinner fall successfully at night you must fish a short leader with a stout tippet in order to fish blind in these dark environs.

Jessie Lake is also productive walleye water, although at the time of this writing walleye are still protected as a result of a population crash in the 1970s.

Above Jessie Lake, which accounts for approximately 10 kilometers of the Nipigon, is an 8-kilometer stretch of the river that flows through a scenic canyon, at times three- to four-hundred feet high. Within this stretch are several hotspots for brook trout in the sixteen- to twenty-four-inch range (two to eight pounds), most of which are near portions of faster current and underwater structure. In addition, catches of lake trout and whitefish are common in this area. Both species attaining respectable size: lakers up to ten pounds, and whitefish up to seven or eight. This stretch of canyon water ends at Pine Portage, the top dam on the Nipigon.

Upstream of Pine Portage Dam is where many of the largest brook trout are still taken on the Nipigon system. Indeed the earliest accounts of big fish—including the record fish—come from places known as Virgin Falls and Rabbit Rapids, which are situated at the top of the river almost 20 kilometers north of Pine Portage. These famous spots are still there, although the original river bed is many feet below the present water level. Consistent with the other dams on the river, the portion of river above Pine Portage Dam is a lake-like portion of the river. This very large lake is known as Forgan Lake. It runs to the northwest as the river proper runs northeast. This situation makes the boat ride to the Virgin Falls area a

Nipigon River Brook Trout
Trout Weight Determined from Length and Girth Measurements

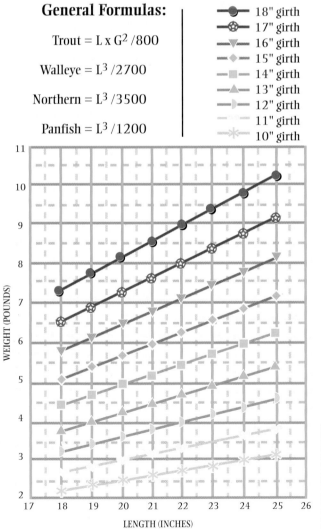

General Formulas:

$$Trout = L \times G^2 / 800$$

$$Walleye = L^3 / 2700$$

$$Northern = L^3 / 3500$$

$$Panfish = L^3 / 1200$$

- 18" girth
- 17" girth
- 16" girth
- 15" girth
- 14" girth
- 13" girth
- 12" girth
- 11" girth
- 10" girth

Bryan Broderick with a typical, thick-bodied Nipigon River brook trout.

COURTSEY OF KURT MELANCON

treacherous ride in windy weather. Subsequently, it is best to travel in a larger craft from Pine Portage north. As one would expect, the rewards available in the Virgin Falls area, just below Lake Nipigon, can be awesome, both in catch and scenery.

Not unlike hot apple pie and ice-cream after a long day's fishing, I've saved the best part of this chapter for the end: the brook trout itself.

The brook trout of the upper Nipigon are a sight to behold. They are beautifully detailed like no other fish I have ever seen. Brilliant orange spots with striking blue halos are the signature markings of these fish. They appear silver in the water, especially on a sunny day, but once you examine them closely, as you gently pull the hook from their mouth and prepare to release them, you will notice their matchless, breathtaking beauty.

As I mentioned previously, they are very thick in the body, especially the denizens of the upper river. So much that regular formulas for calculating a trout's weight do not apply to these brook trout. Rather, a special formula—detailed in this book on a chart developed by ardent Nipigon angler, Kurt Melancon of Minneapolis—is used to calculate the astounding weight of these spectacular brookies. Using this formula, I have found the weight of some brook trout I've caught to be close to seven pounds, even though they were only twenty-one or so inches long. They are not, however, chunky to the extent of being portly or sluggish. In fact, they remain streamlined for their size and fight with a vengeance; eager to run far into your backing in the big river.

This large girth-to-length proportion is naturally due to the amount and type of feed in the river. It would be interesting to compare the proportions of these modern fish to those that existed prior to the damming of the river.

Hatches and Flies

I would suggest that the bulk of the large brook trout on the Nipigon River are duped by large streamers. By far the most successful streamers fished by Nipigon River guides and anglers are varying concoctions of the Strip Leech pattern developed by Gary Borger. These rabbit-strip patterns are tied up to 3 1/2 inches long, on 3X long streamer hooks in sizes 4, 2, and even 1/0. My favourite combination for the river is a

A fly angler works some dry-fly water on the Nipigon River, below Pine Portage Dam.

natural-coloured beige or olive rabbit strip with a chartreuse tail and a gold tinsel body. I add gold Krystal Flash to the tail and a red throat, and tie the pattern with two layers of wrapped lead. It is a formidable looking creature for sure, but when you consider the number of large prey items in the river, such as sculpins and crayfish, it is logical to fish such big patterns. In addition, the needs of any fish dictate that there is no sense expending great amounts of energy to consume what amounts to an hors d'oeuvre-sized offering, after swimming great distances through deep, fast water. I like the pattern I mentioned above because it works for me, but also because I feel it accurately—or at least accurately enough—represents sculpins and also fleeing crayfish. In addition to large sculpins, which are the favoured diet of the Nipigon brook trout, crayfish are very abundant along the rocky shores of the Nipigon, and when moving about on the bottom, scoot along backwards and often upside-down from one lie to another in the current. Brook trout target these substantial fellows and take them quickly before they disappear under a rock. This is also one of the reasons I like to fish these rabbit-strip flies near the bottom with a pulsating retrieve.

Sometime when you're shuffling about along a rocky river-bottom, kick up a few decent-sized stones and look for fleeing crayfish. You will note how they swim backwards and flip upside-down in the current as they scamper downstream to the next available cover. This little experiment will help you understand the merits of fishing these big flies in such a fashion near the bottom.

Although wool-head sculpin patterns, such as my Green-Butt Monkey mentioned in Chapter 1, fish well on the Nipigon, I find that often their bulky heads hamper my attempts to get the fly deep as quickly as possible.

In addition to the rabbit-strip family of flies for the Nipigon, the ubiquitous Woolly Bugger works equally well in the river. Nipigon-Buggers should be tied very large, size 4 or 2, and heavily weighted. Black and brown are the best colours as there are both black and brown phases of large sculpins—or cockatouches as they are locally known—in the river.

Specifically, there are two large sculpin species prevalent in the Nipigon River: the mottled sculpin (*Cottus beirdi*), and the slimy sculpin (*Cottus cognatus*). Both of these species, which are almost identical in appearance, average three inches in length, but can approach five inches in length, which speaks to the success of large streamer patterns for brook trout on this river.

Just about any type of popular dry will work at one time or another on the Nipigon; but I would say the bulk of your selection should consist of caddis patterns, large mayfly patterns, and searching patterns, such as the Royal Trude and the Stimulator. I like fishing size 8 and 10 Yellow Stimulators on the river, because they are easy to see and follow, especially on long casts and drifts, and also because they represent so many different potential food sources: stoneflies, large mayflies, and terrestrials such as hoppers and crickets, which are prevalent during late summer. Although I have never given it a try, I'll bet a mouse pattern will work like dynamite when fished off the edge of the many rock cliffs along the river. One nice thing about brook trout, if they're hungry they'll eat almost anything. On the other hand, if they're not hungry, they can be a real pain in the ass to catch.

One of the most significant hatches of insects on the upper Nipigon is the salmonfly (*Pteronarcys dorsata*), a large species of stonefly that thrives amongst the boulders along the banks and islands of the river. They have creamy-yellow bodies with a band of yellow or orange on their heads. These giant stoneflies are generally two and one-half to almost three inches in length and can often be found drying their wings on rock islands after the nymph has crawled out of the water and fastenied itself to a rock to metamorphose into a winged insect.

One sunny afternoon in late May I pulled my boat onto a tiny island in the river above Jessie Lake and found hundreds of *Pteronarcys* crawling from under the rocks as the sun warmed the island. In addition to the effects of the early afternoon sun, the warmth of my Coleman stove also attracted the stoneflies adding an "extra-special" ingredient to my chicken-stir-fry. Stoneflies gradually left the island as their wings completely dried, however few of them made significant progress as they were soon picked off in mid-air by cruising sea gulls.

Because of the fact that these insects hatch off rocks and not off the water, I believe their true value to the fly angler comes when they return to the river to lay their eggs. This is when they become significant to the trout population. Their large size attracts even the largest brook trout to the surface.

In addition to the *Pteronarcys,* other significant insects on the river include the *Hexagenia limbata,* which thrives in the silt-bottomed areas above the dams and in the lake-like portions of the river. They appear as large (approximately two inches long) greenish-bodied mayflies that hatch after dark in slow-moving sections of river. Most times both duns and spinners are present on the water, specifically just above and just below dams. Brown drakes (*Ephemera simulans)* may be the most beneficial hatch as they appear at dusk and make for some memorable dry-fly fishing. One of my favourite patterns for both brown and gray drakes is the Usual: a simple fly constructed solely from the hair of a snow shoe hare's rear foot. The fly has great buoyancy properties and it floats in the surface film as a hatching mayfly would. I have caught numerous brook trout in the twenty-inch range during this hatch on Usuals.

Grannom caddis hatches are also very important to the Nipigon fly angler. Nipigon's fish seem to have a special lust for caddisflies. They are also present in varying numbers throughout the year.

Some less-significant hatches on the river include the Yellow Sally stonefly, and various other smaller species of stoneflies.

The best timing for prolific hatches of caddis, mayflies and stoneflies is generally the last two weeks of June and the first two weeks of July. August can prove tough fishing if the water temperature reaches above the sixty-five degree mark. Towards the end of August however, nighttime temperatures drop significantly and the water begins to cool once again; brook trout begin to feed with regularity prior to their spawn in late September and October. Good dry-fly fishing in the evening can be had even in September on the Nipigon.

As for presentations, I would say the majority of the takes I have had on dry flies on the Nipigon River have been on the downstream drift of the fly. I like to cast quartering upstream with a large reach mend, and then mend heavily—to flip the fly line upstream of the fly and the leader—as it passes perpendicular to my position. I then allow the fly to drift drag-free downstream ahead of the fly line and leader, at times paying out extra line to lengthen the drift. I have hooked fish with almost the entire fly line on the water on some of the flatter sections of river; hence my tendency to fish larger, more visible dries on the Nipigon.

Recommended Services:

(Refer to Appendix B for addresses and phone numbers.)

Superior Fly Fishing (refer to Chapter 1.)
Guided trips on the Nipigon River are provided by Superior Fly Fishing from May until November. Brook trout are targeted from mid-May to the end of brook trout season in September. Rainbow trout, summer steel-head, lake trout and whitefish are also encountered during this time frame in certain sections of the river. Chinook salmon and steelhead trips are profitable in the fall.

River's Edge Fly Shop (refer to Chapter 1.)
River's Edge also offers similar guide service on the Nipigon River.

A Nipigon brook trout rests briefly after being released.

CHAPTER 10

The Blue Lake System

A Kirkpatrick Lake rainbow trout.

L ike many fly anglers, I have a penchant for fishing rivers. I suppose in a practical sense, moving water is easier to read and dissect into fishable portions than still waters, but more significantly the real attraction is in the constant flow and movement of rivers that provides a soothing, mystical enchantment for the angler. But if you become drawn into the habit, as I have, of always fishing rivers and streams, you can miss out on the tranquillity of fly fishing lakes and ponds, which in their own way provide the same benefits to the angler.

Until recently, I have not spent a great deal of time fishing lakes and ponds. This is quite ironic considering that I live in a region of Northern Ontario that is inundated with small, isolated lakes teeming with eager trout. Other than my penchant for fishing rivers, I guess my only other excuse is that there are just so many trout lakes to fish I don't know where to begin.

In Northern Ontario there exists an innumerable number of wilderness trout lakes primarily inhabited by wild, indigenous populations of brook trout and lake trout. These lakes are in either the Great Lakes or Hudson-James Bay watershed and range from the most westerly drainage of Lake Superior to the Quebec border. In the extreme north they are found anywhere within the Hudson-James Bay drainage. In order to explore and fish these waters, one needs to delve into the reams of stocking and habitat maps and literature available from the Ontario Ministry of Natural Resources, or employ a reputable guide or outfitter, to get a sense of direction for your explorations. To write about these numerous lake opportunities requires a book in itself. Moreover, identifying some of these relatively small and fragile waters specifically, could lead to their ultimate demise. Suffice it to say, that if one wishes to spend some time, effort and money, there is an abundance of wild, trophy trout to be had in Northern Ontario, especially for those who are of hardy stock, and handy with a compass and a paddle.

Having said all that, there are some lake fisheries that are accessible, substantial in opportunity, and managed with enough paternal diligence that they are outstanding in their league. One such fishery is the Blue Lake system.

The Blue Lake system is a series of coldwater trout lakes about 160 kilometers northeast of Sault Ste. Marie, Ontario, in the Lake Huron watershed. This system of five interconnected lakes—Kirkpatrick (Blue), Elbow, White Bear, Robb and Townline—is joined together by the West Little White River, which flows into the Mississaugi River and ultimately into the North Channel of Lake Huron. The system has its own unique and inherent qualities that make it different from most trout fisheries in Northern Ontario. Unlike most trout systems in this region with indigenous populations of brook trout and lake trout, the Blue Lake system was originally devoid of trout until after the area was completely logged in the 1940s. At that time the lakes were stocked with brook trout, lake trout and rainbow trout, and over the years these species have developed into a self-sustaining, totally wild population. The clear, cold, deep waters of these lakes are productive and suitable habitat for exceptional populations of these species. Although each lake has a favourite, brook trout and rainbow trout up to seven pounds and lakers in the low teens can be encountered all through the system. What makes the Blue Lake system significantly unique is the existence of a natural population of rainbow trout in a lake system, which is almost unheard of in Ontario (apart from the Great Lakes).

Kirkpatrick Lake—originally dubbed "Blue Lake" because of its aqua-clear appearance from the air—is the mainstay of the system and the base for Blue Fox Camps, a resort owned and operated by Dr. Paul Morgan, an orthodontist based in Toronto. Morgan, who purchased the camp in 1992, has a particularly paternal, custodial interest in the area. He is

Guide Dave Jackson on the West Little White River at the outlet of Kirkpatrick Lake in the Blue Lake system.

A beaver house in the Blue Lake system.

The dock at Blue Fox Camp.

keenly interested in exposing his operation to the fly-fishing market, and promotes catch and release and other conservation ethics continually. In addition, Morgan is in the development stages for establishing a Native Leadership course at the camp during the off-season.

Kirkpatrick Lake is about eleven miles long, relatively narrow and very deep. The deepest section of the lake is 220 feet deep, and much of the rocky shoreline drops quickly off into depths that one would normally measure in fathoms. There are some spectacular cliffs along the north shore of the lake, some as high as 300 feet. Huge submerged boulder fields along these shorelines are readily visible in the crystal-clear depths to 30 feet and provide ideal cover for trout. Subsequently, the best approach for fishing this type of water is to troll along the shoreline in a 14- or 16-foot aluminum boat powered by a small outboard motor, with one angler working a fly right up against the shore and the second angler, usually the guide, simply trolling a fly on a full-sinking line 100 feet or so behind the boat. Indeed, this is the type of fly fishing I did for the majority of my angling time during my four-day excursion in June of 1998 on the Blue Lake system.

The first trout of my trip—a healthy twenty-inch rainbow—came almost by accident. My inveterate fly-fishing guide Dave Jackson (who even has a Royal Wulff fly tattooed on his chest) and I had been working the northern shore of Kirkpatrick Lake when my fly—a large olive Rabbit Strip Leech—became lodged on the bottom. I had just finished freeing my fly from a cluster of large boulders and was stripping it back to the boat when the fish struck. It was a sleek and strong specimen of a rainbow that put up a fight worthy of its counterparts anywhere in the world.

Naturally, and consistent with lake fishing philosophies for other species, we spent considerable time casting in this area after landing this fish. In fact, each time I had the opportunity to fish Kirkpatrick I hooked up with either rainbow trout or lake trout in this particularly fishy-looking stretch of water.

Although during the dog days of summer lake trout frequent the deeper environs of the lakes, most often in the early and late summer periods lake trout are encountered with exceptional frequency amongst shoreline structure. Lake trout, although not typically thought of as fly-fishing fare, provide great sport on a fly rod, and eagerly take Woolly Buggers, Strip Leeches and just about any other large streamer pattern you can offer them. Contrary to their behaviour when hooked very deep on down-rigger systems, they put up an enviable fight along shoreline environs. They fight very much like a brook trout and often sound deep and run considerable distances, especially when hooked on or near reefs and submerged islands. Unlike rainbow trout and similar again to brookies, they rarely jump.

Fishing the other lakes in the Blue Lake system (Elbow, White Bear, Robb and Townline) involves short to moderate hikes from the main lake (Kirkpatrick) to the smaller interconnected lakes where canoes have been strategically cached. The West Little White River, which flows both in and out of Kirkpatrick Lake, is also a productive haunt for rainbows and brookies for those of U.S. that must fish flowing water.

As an added bonus to fishing this area, a collection of prime, trophy brook trout lakes are also accessible by portage and canoe from the main lake. I am sworn to secrecy on the names of these lakes, but I can tell you that they have been given very peculiar names, apparently in an attempt to detract angler attention from them. Numerous brook trout over five pounds are caught and released each year in these lakes; the largest brookie taken at the camp was a whopping seven pounds!

During one hot June day we fished a total of five small lakes and covered an incredible amount of country in about six hours. The longest portage was only 400 yards, and since I was a guest not a guide, I had nothing to carry but my vest and my rod. Fishing these lakes differed greatly from the Blue Lake system as the only species of fish in these lakes are brook trout.

When planning a trip to the Blue Lake area, it is important to remember that this is a fly-in camp, requiring a flight in a bush-plane from either Blind River or Elliot Lake. From most points, connector flights to Sault Ste. Marie or Elliot Lake are offered by smaller airlines. These companies often have rather small baggage weight limits, so your gear bag must contain the essentials without being cumbersome and overweight. A good seven-weight pack rod will cover most of your requirements. You will be casting from a boat or a canoe on lakes, which means that often you'll be punching line into the wind. A good tip is to overload your rod by one or two line weights. This means that you will require less false casting and have better capability for throwing moderate length casts into the wind. A full-sinking line, or a heavy sink-tip, such as a Teeny 350 or 400, will work well for trolling and casting to deep structure. A floating line will also be necessary for dry-fly fishing.

Hatches and Flies

There are hatches of numerous species of mayflies—particularly *Hexagenia*—in all of these waters. Standard mayfly and caddis patterns from size 16 through 8 will suffice for the hatches here. The bulk of your streamer selection should consist of large patterns that are suggestive of chub minnows, leeches, crayfish and small trout. Olive Woolly Buggers in varying sizes are a must, as are olive, tan and black Strip Leeches or Zonkers. Bring plenty of 2 and 3X tippet for streamer fishing. Some anglers claim that streamers should be fished on 5X on these lakes because of the clear water, but I am a bit skeptical on that theory after seeing some of the contraptions that successful spin fishers use on Kirkpatrick Lake.

Additionally, some excellent stream fishing can be encountered in West Little White River, which is a picturesque piece of water that you won't want to miss. I recommend bringing a lighter rod for the White, perhaps something in the 4- to 6-weight class. Although I did not experience good fishing in the river system due to the timing of my trip, Bob Linsenman made a similar pilgrimage a few years ago and caught some rainbow trout in the 18- to 22-inch class on dries in this brisk, cascading stream that was once a float route for harvested timber.

Speaking of timing, fishing the Blue Lake system is worthwhile anytime between May and the end of September, however the most eager biters are encountered in May and early June, and also in September.

Recommended Services:
Blue Fox Camps

Blue Fox Camps is owned and operated by Dr. Paul Morgan. He employs three guides knowledgeable in fly-fishing techniques and, more importantly, in the waterways and forest trails of the area. Quaint log cabin accommodations—some including hot showers—and hearty meals prepared by an excellent cook are all available at the camp. The site also features a small stream with a covered bridge where in season rainbow trout can be observed spawning in the creek-bed below. Fishing on Kirkpatrick Lake is done from small aluminum boats equipped with 10-horsepower motors (bigger crafts are not allowed on the lake); fishing on the other lakes in the region is accomplished from canoes; walk-and-wade fishing is available on the West Little White River. In addition, the camp has several float-tubes available for clients as there is some respectable evening fishing to be had right in front of the camp.

Some excellent stream fishing can be had on the West Little White River.

The Blue-Ribbon Grand

The Grand River as viewed from The Trestle in section 2.

There are numerous examples around North America on how conservationists can convert a relatively insignificant watershed into a blue-ribbon trout stream, the Grand River is Ontario's shining example of just that.

Several years ago the transformation began; thanks to the insight of a group of Southern Ontario biologists and fly anglers. Due in part to the growing angling pressures on other streams, and the desire to diversify area fishing opportunities, this group—comprised of Ministry of Natural Resources biologists Larry Halyk and Jack Imhof, Warren Yerex of Grand River Conservation Authority, and Trout Unlimited representative Walt Crawford—began to look at the productive Grand for a solution. Some experimentation with rainbow trout had occurred on the Grand with marginal success; the fishery was not self-sustaining, rather it was strictly a put-and-take project, and a poor one at that. Many of the rainbow trout stocked migrated downstream and probably became a part of the steelhead fishery in the lower river. The desire was for a riverine strain of fish that would provide sport in the upper river throughout the trout season from late April to the end of September. A biological survey done on the stream showed the river was much better suited for a brown trout population; subsequently a fisheries plan was formulated and submitted by Larry Halyk in 1988. This resulted in an extensive stocking initiative, beginning in 1989, from a variety of hatchery sources. In 1993, special regulations were placed on a 13-kilometer stretch of the Grand making it catch-and-release (single-hook-barbless, artificials only). Today this stretch of easily waded and accessed stream rivals the best tailwater fisheries anywhere, and is affectionately referred to as the "Blue-Ribbon Grand." Presently strains from other rivers in Southern Ontario are being introduced into the system to further broaden the genetic base for the Grand River population. Some successful spawning does occur, but at this time, the majority of the brown trout caught are stocked fish. This trend will hopefully change as concerned parties, such as the Friends of the Grand River and several fly-angling groups, along with the Grand River Conservation Authority and the M.N.R., are presently developing water quality and spawning area enhancement plans.

This blue-ribbon section I speak of is just north of the city of Guelph. Shand Dam on Belwood Lake, just 5 kilometers north of the town of Fergus, is the source of the tailwater fishery. The dam was modified for hydroelectric purposes in 1988 resulting in a cold-water discharge. This factor, combined with the natural occurrence of cold-water upwellings and the high-nutrient qualities of the river, makes the Grand a prolific trout stream. Abundant hatches of virtually every important insect to the sport of fly fishing are well represented in this upper section of river. Further, the nutrient values of this stream have been augmented by the upgrading of sewage-treatment practices within the catchment area of this system over the last ten years, an area populated by an astounding

730,000 people. This high-population living within the drainage is really a good thing. As explained by G.R.C.A. representative Warren Yerex, the Grand River drainage is the largest populated area in Canada that is dependent on a singular source of ground-water from a river for its water consumption needs. Most urban areas draw from large bodies of water—such as the Great Lakes—for their water source. Given that the Grand is also used for the treatment of sewage for the majority of the inhabitants in the drainage, water quality becomes a very important issue for everyone—anglers and consumers alike. This results in a plus-plus situation. Consumers demand high water quality, hence sewage treatment systems are continually being upgraded, resulting in increasingly better water quality in the river. This is good for the brown trout, and fly anglers as well. The whole circle sounds a little distasteful, but it is a fact of life in populated areas. The issue of human effluent being a boon to a trout population is one of the 'R-rated' factors behind the scenes on many a blue-ribbon trout stream.

All told, there are three sections of catch-and-release brown-trout water on the Grand. Section 1: approximately 2.5 kilometers from the West Garafraxa 2nd line to Scotland Street in the town of Fergus; Section 2: approximately 5.5 kilometers, between Tower Street in Fergus to Bissel Dam in the town of Elora; and Section 3: approximately 5 kilometers, from 100 meters downstream of the "low-level" bridge in the Elora Gorge Conservation Area to 100 meters upstream of the Pilkington 2nd line.

Although these areas are marked with signs, the parameters of these borders likely mean beans to you at this point, unless you're sitting with a detailed map on your lap. Notwithstanding, if you're like me and need

An old mill on the Grand River.

Guide Barney Jones fishes the Grand River faithfully.

one of those "You Are Here" shopping-mall signs when you're standing on the banks of a strange river, you are best advised to employ a guide, at least for your first few trips. Indeed the benefits of hiring a guide on any renowned trout stream are numerous: you want to be sure to spend your time fishing the best water; to make sure you are legally fishing, and not on private property or sanctuary water; and to ensure that you are fishing the right flies, in the right manner, at the right time of day. These reasons are so true for the Grand. Knowledgeable guides—such as John Valk and Barney Jones of Grindstone Angling Specialties in Waterdown, Ontario—know the river intimately. They not only know which stretches hold the biggest fish, the most fish, and the toughest-to-hook fish, they even know their names! Like many brown-trout rivers, the Grand has those ageless denizens of certain pools that inspire that reverie and gossip that is familiar to any fly shop. A good guide has the goods on when the big seven-pounder was last hooked at Blondies (in Section 3) and what it was hooked on. This likely means that this big fish won't take the same pattern again, at least for a while. Good guides are priceless on the Grand for all of these reasons.

I've mentioned the 13 kilometers of special regulation water, but in 1999 the Ontario government introduced legislation to double the amount of special regulation water on the Grand River. This additional water is broken into two sections, which begin downstream of section 3. Section 4, approximately 5 km of river, begins 100m downstream of Pilkington 2nd Line and continues to 100m upstream of the Pilkington Township and Woolwich Township boundary line. Section 5, the longest section of special regulation's water (8 kilometers), starts 100m downstream of the Pilkington Township and Woolwich Township boundary line and continues downstream to a point 100m upstream of Highway 86 (about 2 kilometers upstream of the town of West Montrose). Naturally, anglers that are unfamiliar with these boundaries would be wise to employ a guide, or at the very least refer to a current copy of the Ontario fishing regulations and a good regional road map.

Special regulations now apply to almost all of the 28 kilometers of tailwater/brown trout water on the Grand River from Shand Dam downstream to the picturesque town of West Montrose where the last covered

bridge in Southern Ontario crosses the Grand. This 28-kilometer tailwater section is divided, in geographical terms, into two sections of river: The upper river flows over a bedrock base and through a limestone canyon, known as Elora Gorge, with sheer cliffs up to 100 feet high; and the lower river from the downstream end of the gorge (designated by the bridge that crosses the river there known as the "low-level bridge") to West Montrose. This latter portion of the river has a slower gradient, more occurrences of sand, gravel and upwellings, and a good riffle-run-pool ratio; making this stretch a more classic piece of fly-fishing water as compared to the faster, bed-rock-channeled, upper portion of the stream. These two stretches of river both fish well, but have their own intrinsic differences in hatches and character. The lower stretch is also the area of the river that is best suited for spawning, and may later become a more self-sustaining piece of water. Plans for extending special regulations to include the entire tailwater sections of the Grand are in the works, as are plans to augment spawning habitats in the upper, gorge area of the river.

Fly fishing the Grand is a pleasure. The river averages about 50 feet in width throughout the special regulations area and its flows vary from 140 to 350 cfs. It is pleasantly wadible, and crossed fairly easily in many places. The inherent productivity of the river means there are lots of algae-covered rocks to slip on, so bring your felt soles at the least. I prefer studded-felts for this type of river, as felt alone doesn't always do the trick on snotty rocks. A wading staff is another good measure of prevention.

Any of my fishing compatriots can attest to the fact that I have a propensity for falling in, and inadvertently swimming in, many of the rivers I fish. I could attribute this to a couple of old sports injuries, but mainly it's because I'm usually looking in places other than where my feet are being placed.

The river is ideal for walk-and-wade angling, with lots of access points, trails and crossing points. In addition, the setting is spectacular: lush green ferns and foliage interspersed with yellow and purple blossoms along the banks; Canada geese, deer and mink are regular inhabitants of this same streamside frondescence. All of this gives you the sense that you are in a much more remote place than you really are. The river is nicely sheltered from roads and buildings by forested parklands of cedar and pine. The exception to this is the classic old stone grist-mills along the river. They add character, but also provide for a nice deep pool on the river at their base.

Surprisingly, the river is not crawling with anglers as one might expect. I've seen some interesting spectacles of shoulder-to-shoulder fishing on some other stretches of honey-hole water. But at least when I fished the Grand River I did not get that subtle but persistent feeling that I'd better pee in my waders rather than give up my spot when I moved, like I've sensed in other places. I recall fishing alone one morning on the Article Pool (Trestle area in Section 2) with little competition. I arrived at the river at a leisurely 8:00 a.m., and fished alone until 10:00 a.m. when the first anglers came on scene and courteously circumvented my "place" as they moved downstream. During this time I landed two chunky eighteen-inch browns and a scrappy little ten-incher. Not bad considering I was still within a two-hour drive of the thriving metropolises of Toronto, Hamilton and Mississauga.

I've spent most of my fishing time on the river with John Valk and Barney Jones of Grindstone Angling Specialties. Both men guide on the river and know it very well. John fishes the whole 13 kilometers of special regulations water and follows the hatches and trends from one

The Grand River supports an abundance of insect life in her fertile waters. These nymphs were found beneath one small stone. Following page: A Grand River brown trout taken on a Ttiny nymph.

stretch to another like any good student of a fly-fishing river. John likes the gorge section of the river (between Section 2 and 3) for its resemblance to the Umpqua River Valley, with its sheer cliffs and brisk flows. Because of these same factors—sheer cliffs and brisk flows—this section of the river is not the best place for a beginner. In fact, John will not take clients into the gorge unless conditions are absolutely conducive to safe passage. Once you're in the gorge there is no way out, and purchase along the bedrock bottom of the river is precarious at best. This stretch is also targeted by canoeists, kayakers and sunworshippers, which can be an added pain—unless they're shooting a layout for the *Sports Illustrated* Swimsuit Edition (dream on).

I found the brisker sections of the river more to my liking. I suppose they are reminiscent of the pocket-water streams along Superior's shore that I call home. On the Grand, the faster gradient runs fished well with nymphs, and even better with dries during a hatch. The flatter, deeper, more languid sections of river I found difficult to fish because of, well, difficult fish. The browns in these areas tended to be big "educated" fish that refused even the best presentations. But this is to be expected on any popular trout stream. Trout in flats and slow pools are difficult anywhere you go. John and Barney, however, did not have the same difficulties in hooking fish in these areas; adding that fishing some of these pools was a science in itself. Regardless of your particular tastes for water types, the Grand has it all in a nicely manageable package.

Visibility in the Grand is generally good. It varies from very clear with a slight greenish tinge, to brownish and turbid when it is running high due to a thunderstorm; after which it clears relatively quickly. The visibility also diminishes during the height of the algae bloom in August. This, incidentally, is also the lowest percentage time for hooking larger browns in the river. When I fished the Grand in June, the visibility was clear enough that I could spot large browns flashing on the bottom while nymphing in runs that were about three feet deep. The slight colouration of the water meant that I could still move about on the river without spooking the feeders. This meant that the conditions were just about perfect; clarity changes in either direction would make the fishing much more difficult.

I find this fishing situation quite intriguing:that is to arrive at a stretch of water that at first seems devoid of trout, but some careful examination below the surface, the very reason you're there shows itself from time to time, just enough to keep you focused.

Indeed as I fished the Grand from pool to pool, run to run, day after day, I found myself growing more interested in fishing it as time went on. I wish it was closer to home for me; then again, if it was closer I might find myself spending too much time there. If that is possible.

The brown trout of the Grand River are thick, healthy, strong fish. An eighteen-inch fish is not a big deal, as many fish in the river are in excess of twenty inches. Once the trout reach that size, they seem to grow disproportionately more in girth than length, which is due to the high amounts of available food in the river.

Like any catch-and-release fishery, once the fish reach larger sizes they have likely been caught or hooked before, and for sure have seen their share of feathered hooks. This brings other challenges into play if you are after larger fish. Light tippets, small flies and quick reflexes are in order. Size 12 to 18 nymphs are standard on 4X tippets, while dry flies are generally fished on twelve- to twenty- foot leaders tapering to 5X or 6X. While nymphing the river I no doubt missed ten fish to every one I hooked. The takes are subtle—especially from the larger fish. I learned volumes on nymphing techniques by watching John Valk work the water. He uses his own style of nymph fishing and hooks far more fish than anyone I've fished with. Using an indicator of Biostrike, John fishes small nymphs on a short length of leader below the indicator. His use of added shot is very conservative, even in the faster runs. This is because of how he continually mends and manipulates his line to reduce drag. He uses long rods and carries them in a high position throughout the drift. The key to his hooking success is his inherent ability to keep the line in continual control—keeping a tight line without speeding up the drift— and pulling the trigger on the slightest hesitation or movement of the

indicator. One might assume that many of these movements are weeds or bottom, but in closely watching John fish, I soon noticed that he was fishing considerably less line below his indicator than the total depth of the run. He was still fishing near bottom, but not on bottom. There is a marked difference between the two. If you are fishing with too much added weight or too much leader below the indicator, you will be continuously hung up on weeds and rocks, and ultimately spend most of your time rigging instead of fishing.

The most common rod weight used on the Grand is a 4-weight/nine-footer. Lighter rods will certainly handle the small flies and light tippets required here, but the large size of the Grand's brown trout dictates a good quality four-weight. I used a Sage 3 light-line, 4-weight nine-foot rod and found it just right for the fish, and the moderate casting distances required. If you are going to fish streamers, however, a six-weight would be a better choice.

During my trip to the Grand, John took me to the same favourite haunts that his partner Barney Jones took Jim and Kelly Watt for the production of their video on the Grand River. John made a point of showing me exactly where he hooked and landed a whopping twenty-seven-inch, eight-pound brown in the trestle-area of the river in Section 2. John adds that this fish has been caught both before and after that successful outing. A twenty-five-inch brown was hooked and lost by Kelly Watt during the making of their Grand River video in this same pool. Numerous fish in this size class—and bigger—are in the river. The largest fish landed, to John's knowledge, was a twelve-pound football taken from just below Shand Dam (upstream from Section 1 of the no-kill). This behemoth had been hooked numerous times, but always snapped off after a brief tussle. The size and proportions of this fish were likely attributed to the area in which the fish took up residency; continuously grazing on baitfish and insects that came churning through the turbines at the dam.

As for numbers of fish, no recent electro-fishing has been done, so accurate counts on the population are not available. From my own experience I can tell you that there are plenty. Warren Yerex of GRCA estimates that there are approximately 3000 brown trout per mile throughout the special regulations stretch. This is a raw estimate based on mathematics: 220,000 fish stocked in the last ten years with a 60% mortality rate. Whatever the actual number is, there are quite obviously abundant populations in certain portions of this tailwater stretch.

Hatches and Flies

The single most significant species of insect in the tailwater section of the Grand River are net-building or filtering caddis. The abundance of algae in the river makes it ideal habitat for these insects. According to Ian Martin, an entomology professor and author of *Fly Fishing the Grand River*, the three most important caddis genera on the Grand are the spotted sedge (*Hydropsyche*), the speckled sedge (*Cheumatopsyche*), and the little black caddis (*Chimarra*). The caseless, net-spinning larval stage of these caddis are best imitated by several variations of the caddis larvae nymph pattern in varying shades of green, with or without a bead head. Fishing larvae patterns on smaller hooks, such as size 12-24 TMC 2487, 2457 or Daiichi 1130, is your best bet. The Elk Hair Caddis, Goddard's Caddis and other basic caddis dries in varying colours and in sizes 18 through 12 are good representations of these insects in their adult stage. Hatches of caddis occur from early June through to the end of September, with the largest adults coming off the water earliest in the season and reaching their peak in June.

I witnessed the sheer preponderance of these insects first-hand one evening in June while fishing the low-level bridge stretch (Section 3) with Barney Jones. We had been nymphing a group of large browns that we could see flashing in a nice run between some flats and a large pool. It was about 8:00 p.m. and some caddis could be seen flying around, but the hatch really hadn't come into fruition—at least the fish weren't rising yet. I was busy tying on yet another small nymph when Barney said, "Take a look at your waders." I looked down to see swarms of caddis crawling up the legs of my waders. The entire surface of which, from my thighs to the water level about knee high, was solidly covered with insects. If I wasn't

a fly angler, I would have thought I was in a scene from a Hitchcock flick and gone running up the bank thinking my fate had been somehow horridly sealed. I realized after, that these caddis were not hatching at all, but in the process of laying eggs. We noticed that our wading boots were covered in caddis eggs when we changed at the car later that evening.

In order of abundance, isopods (sowbugs) represent the next food group for the browns. These are crustaceans, or shrimp-like organisms, that do not hatch into flying insects as caddis, mayflies and stoneflies do. They vary in size from approximately size 22 to size 12, but are opaque in colour in contrast to the bright green hues of caddis larvae. Scud patterns using plastic or rubber backs are good representations of the isopod, as are general-utility nymphs such as the Gold Ribbed Hare's Ear Nymph.

One morning on the Grand in June, I began poking around on a small rock island in the river just after the morning bite had subsided. I had noticed several browns flashing in the shallows at daybreak, so I began turning over stones in this particular area. On the bottom of a single softball-sized stone I observed two or three bright green caddis larvae, the same number of sowbugs, and one Hendrickson nymph. I photographed some of them, but couldn't get them all as they were scrambling about in the bright morning light trying to get back into the water. This gave me an instant appreciation of the abundance of food sources in the river.

For the dry-fly aficionado this stream is made-to-measure. The best dry-fly fishing starts around mid-May and continues through July, until the algae bloom reduces visibility. At this point some anglers turn to fishing large crayfish streamers in the coloured water, while dry-fly anglers stick to their guns and fish early morning Trico hatches and spinner falls. I fished the Grand in August and enjoyed some productive mornings during this hatch. My daughter Erin and I picked up several smaller browns on size 18 Griffith's Gnats fishing below the low-level bridge (Section 3).

To follow the hatch chronologically, the festivities begin in mid-May with the Hendricksons (*Ephemerella*), especially in the lower portion of the tailwater. This is followed by the brown drakes in mid-June, with the foxes and cahills (*Stenonema*), *Isonychia* and *Baetis*, coming off through June and July. In addition, a number of stonefly species that were believed to be absent from this stream are now being found in the river. This may be attributed to the ever increasing quality of the water in the system.

To arm yourself properly to conquer the Grand, here are the flies that John Valk recommends as the meat-and-potato dry flies for the river: Hendricksons, Cahills, March Browns and Quill Gordons (orange-tinted hackle) in size 12-16; Blue-Winged Olives in size 12-20; Deer Hair, Elk Hair, and Henryville Special Caddis in sizes 12 through 20; Brown and Green Drake patterns in size 8-12, and Tricos and Griffith's Gnats in 16-22.

The Middle and Lower Grand River

The brown trout, tailwater fishery of the Grand River is only one aspect of this greatly diverse system. The Grand River flows over 236 kilometers from Shand Dam to Lake Erie, gathering size along the way. For most of this length the river is inhabited by smallmouth bass; particularly in the mid-section of the river between West Montrose and Paris, a 100-kilometer stretch of river. This is trophy smallmouth water, with many fish exceeding four pounds in this area. In fact, special regulations for smallies are being considered here, both to augment this population, but also to promote this particular fishery and draw some of the angling attention away from the brown-trout fishery upstream. As many fly anglers are finding out, there is a lot more to fly fishing than trout and salmon.

The bottom stretch of the river below the town of Paris is becoming renowned for its substantial Lake Erie steelhead run in the spring and fall. Incidentally, the steelhead run in the lower Grand may develop into one of the best on Lake Erie, if not Southern Ontario. This new and exciting population is due in part to the same water quality improvements I spoke of earlier, but also because of a change in the upstream barrier to migratory fish on the Grand. In 1988 the Lorne Dam, in the community of Brantford, finally deteriorated to such a point that it blew, making the section above the dam to Paris, accessible to migratory fish. Steelhead began moving into some previously inaccessible nursery waters, such as Whitemans Creek, and recently the system has started to produce some

A nice Grand River brown taken on a dry fly.

respectable steelhead returns. Ontario Ministry of Natural Resources biologist, Jack Imhof, explains that previously this section of the Grand had few steelhead to speak of because of the barrier formed by the Lorne Dam. The stretch below the dam, being a sedimentary warmwater system, did not provide proper conditions for spawning.

Angling pressure and attention on species such as pike, catfish, garpike and smallmouth bass in the lower river add to the survival rate of steelhead smolts traversing this stretch of the Grand to Lake Erie. To further add to this fairy tale, the Grand River receives a late-summer run of steelhead that eat dry flies. John Valk and some of my other steelhead-crazed friends like Rick Kustich and Larry Halyk, have been hooking these exciting steelhead on Bomber patterns, and even size 14 caddis dries. Not just baby steelhead either, fish up to twelve pounds!

Alternate Species

As I have previously alluded to, there are a number of species native to the lower and middle Grand River. The mooneye, a small panfish resembling a perch, populates the lower river in substantial numbers. They have a penchant for feeding off the surface; subsequently they become natural victims to fly anglers. In addition, garpike, northern pike and catfish, are taken on flies as well in this section, although the tackle is substantially more brawny for these species.

Over the years I have come to the conclusion that pious fly fishers will find a way to catch anything that swims on fly gear, rather than turning against their faith and flinging a spoon or any other similarly dubious means of angling.

Recommended Services

Grindstone Angling Specialties

Owned and operated by John Valk and Barney Jones in Waterdown, Ontario, Grindstone (905/689-0880) is a full-service fly shop with a complete stock of flies, fly-tying materials and quality rods, reels and components. In addition, the shop has a guide service, presently with a number of competent and qualified guides, most of whom I have fished with and found to be knowledgeable and excellent company on the river. Their specialties include the Grand River, which constitutes the majority of their guiding business during trout season.

Grand Guides Co-op

The Grand Guides Co-op is a guide service based in Kitchener (519/576-2636) that specializes in full-service guiding to fly anglers on the Grand River tailwaters and other places, as mentioned in this book.

Grand River Troutfitters

A full service Orvis shop in the town of Fergus, Troutfitters (519/787-4359) has an ideal location for catering to Grand River trout bums. The shop also operates a guide service that specializes in Grand River trips.

Journey's End Motels

This Canadian corporation operates seven motel chains in Canada with 100 motels in Ontario. The Sleep Inn, Comfort Inn, Quality Inn, Clarion Inn, Friendship Inn, Econo Lodge, and Rodeway Inn are all operated by Journey's End. These establishments are well maintained and highly recommended by travellers. For the travelling angler these establishments provide clean and affordable accommodations in close proximity to most destination spots. I stayed at the Guelph Comfort Inn (519/763-1900) and found that I was close to all sections of the special regulations water on the Grand and to other Southern Ontario streams and attractions. Comfort Inn has motels in Hamilton, Burlington, Kitchener, Waterloo and Cambridge, which are all in close proximity to the Grand. (For further information on Journey's End Motels refer to appendix 'B'.)

Crimson Maples

Crimson Maples is a quaint bed-and-breakfast in the town of Waterdown operated by Judy and John Bastedo, just a few blocks from Grindstone Angling. Judy is flexible in breakfast times and ensures that everything is neat as a pin when you arrive. The first morning I awoke at Crimson Maples my attention was drawn to the subtle but incessant clattering coming from the downstairs kitchen. When I finished my shower and made my appearance, the spread on the breakfast table was like something you'd see in a magazine: European waffles and trim sausage in abundant amounts, sliced fresh strawberries, fresh-squeezed orange juice, and strong Columbian coffee braced the table—at least momentarily.

I've stayed at Crimson Maples several times and have always had a great breakfast to start the day, something different every time. Judy will make bag lunches on request as well.

Even with such splendid morning fare, the cost of accommodations at this B&B are very reasonable, amounting to what you would pay at most motels—without the breakfast.

Southern Ontario Trout Streams

The Upper Credit River

The special regulations trout waters of the Upper Credit River are situated roughly 45 kilometers northwest of the City of Mississauga (which to tourists seems a western suburb of sprawling metropolitan Toronto). The appearance of the terrain in these headwaters, however, has no semblance to anything urban. In fact, the area looks very pristine and remote with its high hills and dense pine forests. The Credit River originates from groundwater sources in the high, forested bluffs of the Niagara Escarpment—a huge fault that runs across the southern tail of Ontario.

In this area of the Credit system, natural populations of brook trout still flourish. These are remnants of a thriving brook trout population that was once indigenous to the entire Credit River system. This population crashed in the late 1800s, at about the same time the indigenous Atlantic salmon population disappeared from the Credit and other Lake Ontario tributaries. The brook trout population survived this crash and are still wild in the upper system. The Atlantics, unfortunately, did not make the same recovery; however stocking initiatives to re-establish these wonderful salmon, have been in place since 1988.

Between 1938 and 1962, brown trout were introduced to the Credit and established a "wild," self-sustaining population in this upper region of the river. The existence of wild brown trout and brook trout in

Roy De Giusti fishes his beloved Credit River (The Forks of the Credit).

a rugged, pristine, semi-mountainous setting, combined with special angling regulations, makes the Upper Credit a welcoming oasis for urban-bound fly anglers.

The Forks of the Upper Credit

From the gate of The Forks of the Credit Provincial Park, north approximately 10 kilometers to Highway 24 is a provincially legislated stretch of special-regulation water (single barbless hook, no organics). Only one trout exceeding 50 centimeters (about 19.5 inches), may be harvested by an angler in one day.

The river in this area is a moderate to brisk flow with a nice combination of riffles, runs and pools. It has some freestone sections and also some spring-creek like areas with sandy bottoms and grassy overhanging banks. It is just the kind of water you would envision as perfect for trout. There are a number of spring upwellings along the river, which appear as bald spots on the gravely bottom of this clear, aqua-coloured

river. The Credit, in this vicinity, averages about twenty feet in width, with some large pools approaching seventy-five feet. There is plenty of cover for trout provided by large boulders, cedar sweepers, log-jams and overhanging banks. Many pools are chest deep; some are over your head; all are mysteriously inviting to the angler.

I fished this stretch of the Credit on an overcast day in June with Roy De Giusti, a bamboo rod maker, exquisite fly tier, and a devout student of the Upper Credit. We met at a prearranged spot—Eddy Shack's Donuts in the Village of Caledon. (Any of you NHL hockey fans from the original-six era will be quite familiar with the flamboyant Shack, who pestered rival teams and entertained Toronto fans for over a decade in the late 60s and early 70s.) From here I followed Roy in my 4Runner through the Hamlet of Cataract (the town where the cliché "don't blink or you'll miss it" originated), and up some very steep, forested hills. I was amazed at how quickly the countryside changed from rolling fields to towering forest in such a short drive. As we arrived at The Forks of the Credit Provincial Park, Roy referred to some hairpin turns on a hillside switchback that we had just passed, and advised that several car companies have filmed commercials on those very bends. I parked, slipped on my waders and began my pilgrimage at The Forks with Roy as my guide.

The Forks is, as you might have guessed, a fork in the river at the confluence of the main and west branches of the Credit River. The water immediately at the forks is fairly shallow and nicely enveloped with a canopy of maples. Upstream from the Forks, on the main branch, is where the special-regulations water is situated. It immediately deepens into a series of runs and pools from here north approximately 10 kilometers to the bridge at Highway 24, which defines the upper limit of this section. Roy and I fished a substantial portion of this stretch for the majority of the day. The overcast conditions were perfect for midday angling; but alas, we did not land any browns. However, we each landed a few eight-inch brook trout on Roy's Isonychia Nymph, and some small rainbow trout that were actually steelhead smolts. Roy explained that some steelhead are getting over the Norville Dam and gaining access to the trout section. This concerns many of the fly anglers who frequent this stretch, as it is believed that the steelhead will in time have an effect on the wild, resident browns and brook trout.

As we worked upstream, Roy gave me his complete analysis of the Upper Credit, explaining in detail the critical hatches, the best holding lies and the quirks of the large wily browns that inhabit the best hide-outs in the river. At one nice bend he instructed me to take a small trail that circumvented the river so that I would not "spook the pool" as I made my approach—which had to be on my hands and knees as I got into final position on a small clump of weeds along the bank. Roy explained that there is usually at least one large brown in this pool, but normally the first few drifts will result in takes from brook trout and rainbows, after which—if you were lucky—the big brown would take. I casted one of his lifelike Isonychia Nymphs into the head of the pool and mended once as per his instructions. On that drift I picked up a small brook trout, as I did on the next two casts. Over the next thirty minutes I picked up a few more small brookies and rainbows. Then the activity stopped. Roy had been right on the money with his predictions so I braced myself for the big cahuna. It showed. But my reflexes were hampered by an untimely brain fart and I missed the take, and a faint, large, yellowish form became the closest I would get to a big brown that day.

Roy had a refusal from a bantam-weight brown on a Yellow Sally dry and explained that the wild browns in the Credit are typically particular, requiring a perfect representation and presentation for success. This, no doubt, is why Roy's patterns are so life like. Particularly his series of stonefly dries, which are so real in appearance people have a tendency to photograph them rather than tie them on the hook.

The discerning nature of these wild browns is what provides the allure to this stretch of trout stream for Roy De Giusti. He has caught several browns in the eighteen- to twenty-two-inch class here, and had some productive days when conditions were just right. The browns in this stream have a more clean and wild appearance than their counterparts in the Grand River, especially towards the end of September when the browns don their brilliant spawning colours.

Fishing and wading along the Upper Credit I couldn't help noticing how fishing this river seemed reminiscent of some of the videos I have watched on fly fishing New Zealand streams. Roy would continually stalk along the bank as we approached known holding stations for browns, and direct my positioning and casts. It seemed the kind of stream that would not fish well if you were careless in your approach to any productive-looking water.

Although the trails along this stretch were well worn, we did not encounter any other anglers that day. Roy finds himself alone on the Credit quite often; as many anglers flock to the Grand for high-percentage fishing.

As a side note there is a 25-kilometer trail connecting the Forks of the Credit with the Grand River. From that end it can be picked up near the trestle in Section 2.

Hatches and Flies

June is the month for dry-fly fishing on the Upper Credit, as it is in most parts of Ontario. The important hatches begin with the sulphers (*Ephemerella dorothea* and *invaria*) in late May, followed by the green drakes (*Ephemera guttulata*) and yellow sallies (*Isoperla*) during the first week in June. Mid-June marks the arrival of the best hatches including the giant drake (*Hexagenia limbata*), golden stoneflies (*Acroneuria lycorias*, *Paragentina media* and *Phasganophora capitata*) and the *Isonychia bicolor*, which is very prolific on this stream.

Patterns for these important hatches vary from angler to angler but the following are proven patterns on the stream: For nymphs ensure you include the ubiquitous Gold Ribbed Hare's Ear Nymph (which produces very well in early season) in sizes 18 through 12; Ray's Isonychia Nymph in sizes 10, 12 and 14; and lastly a very simple tie—Walt's Worm, also known as the Food Nymph.

This exceptionally simple fly, consisting of just Hare's Ear Plus, gray or brown dubbing wrapped on a small nymph hook, is uncanny for duping trout on the Upper Credit and other streams. I missed three or four takes on another nymph when Roy pulled out what appeared to be a chunk of belly-button fluff and had me tie it on my leader. The first drift with Walt's Worm resulted in a tremendously overt take by a fish that ran instantly under a log jam and snapped me off—never to be seen again. The pattern resembles a number of food organisms in the river, and because of its simplistic design is likely not fished often—being written off as not really a fly at all.

Dry flies include size 14 to 18 Yellow Cahills to represent the yellow sally, and Ray's Golden Stonefly in sizes 8 and 10 to represent the remainder of the predominant and abundant stoneflies on the Upper Credit. All of which should be fished low in the surface film (trimmed or hackle-less) for best results.

Other Areas on the Upper Credit

A second special regulations stretch of the Upper Credit River exists just north of the town of Inglewood from the Grange Sideroad bridge (best access point) north approximately 2 1/2 kilometers. This section has identical special regulations to the Forks section, but in contrast this section is managed by the Greg Clark chapter of Trout Unlimited, the Izaak Walton Fly Fishing Club, and the Credit Valley Conservation Authority. This management initiative was developed with the cooperation of landowners adjacent to this section of stream.

This short stretch of river fishes well for brown trout with the same patterns and techniques as the Forks stretch.

Downstream from the Trout Unlimited area of the Credit is open to fishing but regular limits and bait are allowed. Near Inglewood are some slow, deep pools with some very big browns that are wise to hook and worm. They are worthwhile pursuing during the hatch of the largest insects, such as the Hexes and the golden stones.

The Belfountain Conservation Area, which is located on the West Credit River (the westerly branch from the Forks), is renowned for good brook trout and brown trout fishing as well.

Whitemans Creek

Whitemans Creek (also known as Horner Creek) is another classic Southern Ontario fly-fishing stream. A tributary of the Grand River that enters the Grand just north of the City of Brantford, Whitemans is renowned for its wild population of brown trout. In fact, newer brown trout populations in the province, such as the Arrow River and the Grand River, owe their success, at least in part, to brood stock and eggs that originated from Whitemans Creek. A special-regulations stretch of the creek at App's Mill Nature Centre—between Robinson Road and Cleaver Sideroad—offers an excellent fly-fishing opportunity on approximately 6 kilometers of what I would describe as a small-sized and easily managed trout stream.

The brown-trout fishery was first developed on Whitemans about thirty years ago. Consistent with many other brown-trout stockings in the Midwest, browns were introduced to augment failing indigenous brook-trout stocks that once thrived in Whitemans. Brookies are still present, but their numbers are not significant.

Special regulations on Whitemans Creek dictate the use of artificial lures (including flies) with a barbless hook. The daily possession limit is a combination of five salmon or trout with only one from among rainbow and brown trout. These must be a minimum length of 50 centimeters (or 19.7 inches).

I fished Whitemans with John Valk for just one evening in June of 1997 and wished I could have spent considerably more time exploring this clear, brisk-flowing stream. In many ways Whitemans reminds me of the Upper Credit, and even Michigan's Little Manistee, with its abundance of undercut banks, cedar sweepers, log jams and deep bend pools; indeed the hallmarks of any prolific brown-trout fishery. I chose to fish the stretch with a method I employ with great success on my home streams along Superior's Canadian shore, and that is simply tying on a small Muddler Minnow and fishing it both as a dry on the downstream drift and as a wet on the swing at the end of the drift. This allows you to place the fly nicely beneath overhanging cover, which normally would hamper casting efforts to these prime lies. I encountered a few small browns and brook trout (which are always a pleasure to meet) and saw some substantial rises that had to belong to big browns. John showed me several large, deep pools that no doubt hold some big browns and memorable catches when the hatches and your timing are right.

Like all good trout streams, the key to the continued success of this fishery is its excellent water quality, both in nutrient value and water temperature. These same conditions make good nursery habitat for steelhead, which are recently making a resurgence on Whitemans Creek since the destruction of Lorne Dam on the Grand River in 1988. Since that time steelhead from Lake Erie have been able to access the cool and fertile middle stretches of the Grand River and her tributaries, including Whitemans Creek, to spawn. This has greatly augmented the steelhead population in the Grand system, as much of the water below Lorne Dam was rather poor spawning habitat. What this means to the Whitemans angler is that you will encounter steelhead—both adults and juveniles—while fishing for trout. Some anglers suggest this change in occupancy may lead to the further displacement of brook trout in the creek.

Hatches and Flies

Important hatches on Whitemans are very similar to the list for the Grand River, but include more stonefly species due to the faster gradient and existence of coarse gravel; specifically brown and golden stoneflies. One of the most significant mayfly hatches for big fish is the *Ephoron leukon*, or white-gloved howdy, which is present during July and August. Blue-winged olives are a staple food source beginning the second week of June and continuing on a periodic basis throughout the summer. Various caddis species are also present throughout the season.

Like the majority of Ontario streams, the best time for fishing Whitemans is in June and early July. This is when the best dry-fly fishing is encountered. A parachute-style cream variant in sizes 10 to 14 seems to be one of the better patterns for the *Ephoron leukon*. Standard Blue-Winged Olive patterns and Elk Hair Caddis dries in varying sizes and colours should make up the bulk of your dry-fly arsenal for this stream. Stoneflies are more importantly represented as nymphs than they are as adults. Similarly caddis larvae patterns in sizes 12 and 14 are also productive.

Upper Saugeen River

The upper Saugeen is arguably the next fly-fishing hotspot in Southern Ontario. The Saugeen River system is a huge watershed with an abundance of cold, ground-water-fed tributaries in its headwaters that ultimately flows into Lake Huron at Southhampton. These headwaters of the Saugeen boast resident brown trout (both wild and hatchery stocks) up to twenty-plus inches , and indigenous brook trout that run between six and sixteen inches. The prevailing water conditions of the upper Saugeen are characterized by clear, slightly tannic-stained flows, good boulder and bedrock structure, gravel-bottomed riffles and runs, and deep, slow, silt-bottomed pools where great hatches are born. Cold ground water seeps into the Saugeen and its tributaries from the many adjacent cedar swamps in this region of Southcentral Ontario. Watercress is common along the banks and speaks to the fertile nature of this water system.

Although there is virtually hundreds of kilometers of tributaries to fish and explore, the best and most readily accessed fly-fishing areas are contained in the section of the main Saugeen from the town of Durham upstream approximately 20 kilometers to Priceville; the Rocky Saugeen near Highway 6, and the main Saugeen from Paisley upstream to Walkerton—where presently 5,000-10,000 brown trout are stocked annually on an experimental basis. A recent dam removal on the Rocky Saugeen has enriched the lower reaches of this tributary and the stretch downstream of the confluence of the Rocky and main Saugeen near Hanover, by depositing silt throughout. Fly angler, Len Yust, explains that previous to this occurrence the brown trout in this portion of the Saugeen were rather concentrated and easily targeted. Now the trout are more evenly distributed in this area.

Both the Rocky and main-branch Saugeen are quite manageable by walk-and-wade anglers, with the Rocky Saugeen averaging about twenty feet wide and the Saugeen River averaging around thirty feet wide. The main Saugeen boasts larger, deeper pools, with some pools reaching fifty feet in width and over five feet in depth. The main Saugeen can also be fished with a small boat or canoe.

Access points for fishing the Saugeen include the Durham Conservation Area in Durham, and the trailer park off Highway 6 for the Rocky Saugeen.

Presently the previously mentioned sections of the Saugeen can be fished only during the regular trout season in Southern Ontario, which is from the last Saturday in April to September 30.

Hatches and Flies

The main branch and Rocky Saugeen are noted for good hatches of caddis, Hendricksons (*Ephemerella*), sulphers (*Ephemerella dorothea* and *invaria*), March browns (*Stenonema vicarium)*, and blue-winged olives. Brown drakes (*Ephemera simulans)* and *Hexagenia limbata* are found in the siltier regions of the main-branch Saugeen. Good representations of these hatches are nicely covered in the Grand River and Credit River portions of this book.

Beaver River

The Beaver River is another burgeoning trout fishery in southcentral Ontario, which flows into Georgian Bay. The Beaver runs through the scenic Beaver River Valley and like the Saugeen River, has a respectable run of steelhead in its lower reaches. The total length of the Beaver is roughly 45 kilometers; steelhead are found only in the section of the Beaver below the village of Kimberly where an electronic barrier to migratory fish exists. From here upstream to Hog's Falls—

accessed off Lower Valley Road—the river has wild populations of brown trout and brook trout. Upstream of Hog's Falls brook trout are the primary species for fly anglers to target. A small lake in the town of Flesherton was routinely stocked with brook trout in the past and this may be the source of many of the wild brookies in the Beaver today. The headwaters of the Beaver include the Boyne River, which originates in the same highland hills as the upper Saugeen. Subsequently the hatches and fly selection to fish the Beaver is almost identical to that of the Saugeen.

The Beaver River is typified by brisk, lively flows, with lots of pocket water and freestone runs. The Beaver is renowned for plentiful hatches of insects.

Some good locations on the Beaver include Hog's Falls and the area near the Beaver Valley Hydro Commission. Both of these areas are accessed off Lower Valley Road, which runs north from Highway 4.

Cold Creek

Cold Creek is a sweet little tributary of the Trent River system, which flows into the Trent at the town of Frankford. The Trent, in turn, flows into Lake Ontario near the city of Trenton. Cold Creek is strictly a resident brown trout and brook trout fishery due to migratory fish barriers on the Trenton system. The upstream reaches of Cold Creek west of Highway 30 is noted for big browns, eager brookies, and all-around good-looking trout water.

I fished Cold Creek with Bob McKenzie from Oshawa, Ontario, an avid fly angler and manufacturer's representative for Sage, Scientific Angler, and a number of other leading companies in the fly-fishing industry. As you might imagine, fishing with Bob is a bit of a mini trade show in itself, with an abundance of new kinds of tippets, fly tying materials, and the latest in high-modular graphite bouncing about—both figuratively and literally. In any event, Bob is a great fishing companion and an all-around good guy, and although this particular day-trip on Cold Creek did not pay particularly great dividends, I enjoyed a twenty-plus steelhead outing on the Ganaraska during the same week with Bob, so the fish owed me nothing.

Public access on Cold Creek is best from the Goodrich-Loomis Conservation area accessed off Highway 30 (Follow the signs. Take the 401 freeway east from Toronto/Oshawa to Highway 30). There is roughly 10 kilometers of water to fish, and the nature of the river is a meandering freestone stream averaging twenty feet in width, with lots of cedar sweepers, flotsam and undercut banks for cover. There are some slow, deep sections of the river that are known for producing large browns. In fact Bob's largest was a 26 1/2-inch beast (that ate the chub that swallowed his fly—or something to that effect) that came from one of these slow, silt-bottomed sections.

The Cold Creek Flyfishers (a local club) has exclusive access to a section of the creek just upstream of Highway 30. Upstream of this posted area is the section accessed from the Goodrich-Loomis Conservation area. These two sections, for all intents and purposes, contain the best trout waters; although some leviathan browns are found east of Highway 30 in the slower, wider, meandering downstream sections of the river.

Fly selection and hatches are quite similar to those listed elsewhere in this chapter (Upper Credit, Grand River), but give particular attention to the mayfly nymphs and dries in your box, as well as some big baitfish imitations. Crayfish are abundant in Cold Creek; hence crayfish patterns should be fished with faith and persistence. Small brookies, which are also prevalent in this watershed, are also a popular menu item for big browns, so don't be afraid to fish a good-sized streamer in known big-brown haunts on Cold Creek.

Recommended Services:

(Refer to Appendix B for addresses and phone numbers.)

Grindstone Angling Specialties
Grand Guides Coop
Grand River Troutfitters

CHAPTER 13

Exotic Quarry

As I mentioned in the introduction to this book, Ontario boasts an incredibly diverse fishery. This is why—as a fly-fishing addict—I am very glad to live in this part of the world. Within the distance I can travel on one tank of gas from my home in Thunder Bay, I can fish for trophy brook trout (naturally at the top of my list), steelhead (a close second), Chinook, pink and coho salmon, lake trout, brown trout, smallmouth bass, northern pike, walleye, whitefish, musky, perch, carp, and even suckers—which we wryly refer to as "golden bonefish" in fly-fishing circles.

If I extend this radius to encompass the entire province of Ontario (a few more tanks of gas), I can add several more species to this very large list. A few examples would be largemouth bass, mooneye, garpike, catfish—and a subspecies of brook trout found only in Northeastern Ontario known as the aurora trout. There are several species that I have inadvertently overlooked, and hundreds of species of

A male aurora trout from Whirligig Lake in full spawning colours (captured in a MNR research net).

baitfish—some of which will even take a fly—that make this list incomprehensible.

Seriously though, there are a couple of opportunities for rare and exotic fish that are readily available to the travelling fly angler, and very worthwhile of your attention.

Aurora Trout

The aurora trout—at one time thought to be a separate species altogether—is a special, colour-variant subspecies of the brook trout that is indigenous in only two small lakes in Northeastern Ontario near the town of Temagami. These two lakes—Whirligig and Whitepine—are within the boundaries of Lady Evelyn-Smoothwater Provincial Park, and still maintain naturally reproducing populations of auroras. Logically, these two lakes are completely closed to angling. In fact, at the time of this writing aurora trout are listed as an endangered species by Canadian authorities. Despite this, there are nine lakes in surrounding districts that are stocked with aurora trout and provide a unique fly-angling opportunity that cannot be experienced anywhere else in the world!

The aurora trout was first officially discovered in 1923 when a party of Pittsburg, Pennsylvania anglers caught a trout in Whitepine Lake with unique markings and colouration unlike anything they had ever seen before. Apparently, several specimens were preserved in formaldehyde and examined by authorities.

In 1925 a report on this unique trout was published by fisheries biologist A.W. Henn and angler W.H. Rinkenbach. The report concluded that this finding constituted a new species and was dubbed the aurora trout because of its spectacular colouration that rivaled the brilliance of the northern lights (Aurora borealis). The aurora trout was given the species name *Salvelinus timagamensis: Salvelinus* denoting char, and *timagamensis* denoting the limited geographical area in which these fish were found.

It seems logical to authorities that the aurora strain developed about 10,000 years ago when the ice-age forgings of our continent separated these highland lakes from other water-heds in this northeastern region of Ontario near the border of Quebec. The aurora lakes are adjacent to the Ishpantina Ridge—the highest point of land in Ontario—and are sourced by natural, cold upwellings of well-oxygenated ground water; ideal habitat for these wonderful fish.

Fortunately, in the following decades after the discovery of the aurora, fishing pressure was minimal, providing a much needed time cushion for biologists to garner several breeding adults for study and breeding purposes. For once the post-second-war economic boom hit the region, the pristine condition of these two lakes was decimated by acid rain. Specifically the effects of fallout from a newer, larger, effluent stack in Sudbury, Ontario, the predecessors of which had turned Sudbury's surroundings into moonscape, had a catastrophic effect on the aurora trout in these two remote lakes.

Subsequently, our present-day stocks of aurora trout originate from nine individuals—three males and six females—that were extracted from the natural population in a very timely manner!

The birth-place of this saved subspecies of brook trout is the Hills Lake Hatchery near Cochrane, Ontario. Starting in the 1950s this hatchery began producing auroras and still does at the time of this writing. Auroras from Hills Lake Hatchery have been used to stock a number of lakes in the northeastern region of Ontario, and one lake in the Terrace Bay District on the northshore of Lake Superior. The intent of this introduction initiative is two-fold in that the stockings provide for angling opportunity in non-native waters, and make for a backup population should something tragic occur in the native lakes.

Ontario Ministry of Natural Resources biologist, aurora trout specialist and fly angler, Ed Snucins, explains that although angling for an endangered species raises the hackles on some environmentalists, angling opportunity is crucial to the aurora program. Snucins relates that the angler interest fostered through carefully monitored and regulated fishing opportunities on specified put-and-take aurora trout lakes heightens public awareness and interest in the plight of the aurora trout. Simply put, if anglers could not fish for aurora trout—they would soon be forgotten.

The present OMNR aurora trout management strategy is a multi-faceted one:

Firstly, monitoring and sustaining the population in the indigenous lakes—Whirligig and Whitepine—has meant a series of lime treatments since the original liming in Whirligig Lake in 1989 to counteract the effects of acid rain (it was thought that a one-time liming would suffice—but alas this is not the case). No angling is allowed in these two lakes.

Secondly, the stocking of regional lakes to provide an angling opportunity in the general vicinity of the original aurora trout range. Presently there are nine stocked, aurora trout lakes, each having an alternating open season every three years—resulting in three lakes being open to angling each year. The season is from August 1 to October 15, which allows anglers to pursue the aurora when it is decked out in full spawning colours. Since no natural reproduction occurs in these stocked lakes, the concern for spawning interference by angling is nonexistent.

Thirdly, having a source diversity for brood stock is an added measure of insurance in case something tragic occurs in one or more of the indigenous aurora waters. The lake in the Terrace Bay region that was

stocked with auroras, as it turns out, now has a self-sustaining population. This is the only lake where auroras were introduced and reproduced naturally. Again, logically, this lake is completely closed to angling.

Lastly, the OMNR endeavours through its angling and stocking initiatives to increase the awareness of the public regarding the aurora trout. This seems to be working, as writings in angling publications—such as this one—are evidence that this final objective is working.

As an interesting sidebar, the issue of whether the aurora trout is a separate species—as once thought—or a subspecies of the brook trout, is still vigorously debated in angling circles. One interesting fact is that in at least one native aurora trout lake, aurora trout and brook trout coexist and do not interbreed. Some separate-species proponents also argue that the aurora has a number of characteristics that differ from the brook trout—the most obvious being the colouration—but also some maintain that auroras spawn later in the fall than brook trout. This taxonomic debate will no doubt continue for years to come.

Identifying an aurora trout can be a little difficult. At a distance an aurora looks very much like a regular brook trout, but on closer examination you will find that some of the signature markings, of the brook trout are absent: The vermiculations, or worm-like markings on the back of the brook trout that extend to the dorsal and caudal fin are completely absent, as are the signature cream-coloured flank spots of the brook trout. Most auroras do not have the blue-haloed, red spots of the brook trout, but instead have a silver or purplish sheen to them depending on the time of year. The aurora has a dark, tawny-brown or charcoal back which fades into a purplish-green upper side, followed by an ochre tone in the lateral line region. The lower flank region of the aurora is characteristic of brook trout having a splash of pinkish-red on the lower flank, and lower fins with a leading edge of white, followed by a band of solid black and the same signature pinkish-red on the body of the fin. Like brook trout, the male aurora is far more colourful in the fall than the female, with scarlet red flanks, belly and fins. Often the various flank colours of the aurora bleed into one another, which aptly gave rise to its name: the aurora trout. Adult auroras range from one to five pounds.

Catching an aurora trout, like all pursuits in the sport of fly fishing, takes some persistence on the part of the angler. The first step would be to identify which lakes are presently open to angling and then begin planning your pilgrimage.

Guides that specialize in aurora trout are as rare as the fish themselves, but if you extrapolate brook trout angling technology and apply it to the pursuit of auroras you will be in the strike zone. Auroras are a lake fish—not a river fish—so you'll need a canoe or a float tube as a working platform. Concentrate your efforts around shoreline structure, particularly adjacent to deep water. Rocky points and underwater reefs are prime locations.

Aurora trout biologist Ed Snucins informs that the aurora trout is an opportunistic feeder. Stomach content examinations reveal a diet high in aquatic nymphs, particularly dragonfly nymphs, but the fish will also consume crayfish, leeches, and even mice on an occasional basis. During OMNR research outings auroras are caught for scientific analysis routinely by angling with a simple gold spoon. Subsequently, one should be sure to have some large streamers incorporating materials such as gold tinsel chenille or gold Krystal Flash. Because the season for auroras does not open until August—after the best of Ontario's hatches are finished—dry-fly fishing is not as predictable as working a nymph, streamer or wet-fly pattern. Sink-tip and full-sinking lines are great tools for lake fishing and should be considered a necessity when preparing your kit for an aurora excursion.

Fly angler and outdoor writer, Geoff Bernardo from Cavan, Ontario, has spent considerable time fishing and exploring several aurora trout lakes in Northeastern Ontario. Geoff has had success in Carol Lake in the Gogama district with black Woolly Buggers and a fly he calls an Olive Deer Hair Wiggler, a pattern that closely imitates the freshwater shrimp that inhabits Carol Lake. Geoff suggests varying your presentations, flies and techniques for auroras as there is not an abundance of information on fool-proof techniques for these fish. Geoff has spent almost a decade pursuing these spectacular trout and has written articles on his endeavours. He has also been outspoken in his views regarding the proper management and conservation of the aurora.

Presently aurora trout need good friends: anglers that are conscientious in their approach and attitude toward angling. Although the legal limit on aurora trout is only one fish where angling is permitted, illegal harvest of these fish occurs in their remote habitats. Hopefully, the increasing presence of reputable anglers on aurora waters will curb this activity.

Aurora Trout Information

Angling opportunities for aurora trout exist in the following three management districts in Northeastern Ontario:

Gogama District Ministry of Natural Resources
2000 Low Avenue, Box 730
Gogama, Ontario
P0M 1W0
705/894-2000

Kirkland Lake District Ministry of Natural Resources
Box 129, Corner Hwy. 66 & 112
P0K 1T0
Kirkland Lake, Ontario
705/642-3222

Timmins District Ministry of Natural Resources
896 Riverside Drive
Timmins, Ontario
P4N 3W2
705/267-7951

Garpike

I first heard about the offbeat pursuit of fly fishing for garpike while reading an essay by John Gierach, in which he was fishing some tepid waters in the Southern United States. I believe the operative technique was to cast a chunk of frayed, yellow, nylon rope—sans hook—to these prehistoric-looking creatures. The idea of the hookless "fly" is born of the notion that the garpike's mouth is simply too hard to penetrate with a steel hook, subsequently the frayed rope tangling in the garpike's numerous teeth becomes a more logical method of procurement. Not that you want to eat one of these things anyway. In the sport of garpike fly fishing, the enjoyment is more in the hooking than in the landing, it seems.

When I learned that garpike existed—and even flourished—in Southern Ontario I was quite surprised. I was also titillated, because I am equally drawn to such bizarre, difficult and even dangerous pursuits.

Chris Marshall, an accomplished fly angler, writer, and editor/publisher of brand-new *The Canadian Fly Fisher* magazine, has helped pioneer angling for garpike in Southern Ontario. His techniques are very similar to flats-fishing methods used for tropical saltwater fish, such as redfish and bonefish, and involve the same stealthy and observant approach to shallow coastal waters.

Chris makes his home in Belleville, Ontario and enjoys fishing for garpike in the Bay of Quinte in August, when fly fishing for trout and bass is not as productive.

The garpike in Southern Ontario is specifically the long-nosed gar, *Lepisosteus ossius*. It is a long, lean, sickle-shaped predator with an elongated snout and a greenish-silver metallic appearance. It thrives in warmwater shallows where it hunts for baitfish, sunfish and perch. Subsequently, the best way to angle for these fish is to search shallow bays for patrolling garpike and deliver large, flashy streamers in their paths. Chris Marshall prefers large glitzy flies such as the Clouser Deep Minnow in size 2/0, or any other minnow-like streamer constructed with flashy, pearlescent materials. Large orange or yellow Woolly Buggers will also produce. Choose a stiff-action seven- or eight- weight rod; a stiff action is a necessity for driving the hook into the hard mouth of the garpike. Hooks must be extremely sharp and strong; expect to land about thirty percent of the garpike you hook. Their fight is typically short and vigorous with lots of aerobatics. Fish are often lost when they become airborne. Choose a floating line designed for delivering large flies, such as Scientific Anglers' Pike taper, when fishing for garpike.

Garpike, like other large predatory fish, such as musky and northern pike, will follow their prey for some distance before they take. Fly anglers have a natural tendency to stop or slow the retrieve of the fly once this occurs, but Chris points out that you should in fact increase the speed of the retrieve to entice a strike. Garpike will often lose interest in your offering if you decelerate the retrieve.

Garpike typically range between 24 and 48 inches in length, although they will exceed this size in some waters.

Garpike can be found in a number of warmwater environs in Southern Ontario. In addition to the Bay of Quinte, garpike can be found with regularity in Hamilton Bay in Lake Ontario (west end), Honey Harbour in Georgian Bay, and in the lower Grand River near the town of York. In 1976 the catching of a 60-inch garpike was reported in a regional Grand River newspaper. This fish came from the tepid waters of the lower Grand.

Mooneye

This pint-sized member of the shad family has a penchant for dry flies and thus has its own following of fly anglers interested in offbeat adversaries. In fact, the Hamilton Fly Fishers holds an annual mooneye night-fishing excursion on the lower Grand River each summer. This small, silvery, large-scaled, herring-shaped fish averages about twelve inches long and is jokingly referred to as a miniature tarpon in some circles.

The mooneye, *Hiodon tergisus,* is present in considerable numbers in the Grand River from Caledonia downstream to Dunnville. During good hatches of caddis, white millers (*Ephoron leukon*) and other mayflies, dozens of mooneyes can be duped in a single evening on dries fished on a one- or two-weight rod. Elk Hair Caddis in sizes 12 to 18, White Millers in sizes 14 and 16 and size 12 to 16 Usuals are great mooneye patterns.

A good access point on the Grand for mooneye excursions is Seneca Park off Highway 54 in Caledonia.

Appendix A
Fly Shops, Outfitters and Guides

Albert's Fishing Camp
Peawanuck, ON
P0L 2H0
705/473-2507

Blue Fox Camp
8178 Yonge St.
Thornhill, ON
L4J 1W5
416/886-8242

Cedar Point Lodge
General Delivery
Waldhof, ON
P0V 2X0
807/227-2066
www.cedarpointlodge.com

Crimson Maples
155 Main St. North
Waterdown, ON
L0R 2H0
905/689-1097

Eric Dicarlo
Box 1620
Wawa, ON
P0S 1K0
705/856-2802

Fish Tales Custom Tackle
761 River Road
Sault Ste. Marie, ON
P6A 5K9
705/759-9315

The Ganny Fly and Tackle Shoppe
105 Walton St.
Port Hope, ON
L1A 1N4
905/885-9898
www.flyfish.ca

Grand Guides Co-op
"Southern Ontario's Fly Fishing Specialists"
6 Gilkison St., RR2
Elora, ON
N0B 1S0
519/846-8448
www.flyshop.com

Grand River Troutfitters
790 Tower St.
Fergus, ON
N1M 2R3
519/787-4359
www.grandrivertroutfitters.com

Grindstone Angling Specialties
P.O. Box 442
24 Mill St., North
Waterdown, ON
L0R 2H0
905/689-0880

Journey's End Corporation
5000 Explorer Drive,
    6th Floor
Mississauga, ON
L4W 4T9
905/624-9720
Canada-wide directory and
    bookings:
1-800-424-6423
www.hotelchoice.com

Little Inn of Bayfield
Main Street
P.O. Box 100
Bayfield, ON
N0M 1G0
1-800-565-1832
www.littleinn.com

Merkel's Camp
Box 473
Dryden, ON
P8N 2Z2
807/938-6428

Misty Springs Fish Farm
Thunder Bay, ON
P7B 1X6
807/624-6666

Natural Sports
1572 Victoria St., North
Kitchener, ON
N2B 3E5
519/749-1620
www.natsport@golden.net

Rainbow Sports
10 Wyman Rd., Unit 4
Waterloo, ON
N2V 1K7
519/746-2650
1-888-746-2650

Red Rock Inn
Box 525
145 White Blvd.
Red Rock, ON
P0T 2P0
1-800-213-7625

River's Edge Fly Shop
485 Memorial Ave.
Thunder Bay,
ON P7B 3Y6
807/345-3323
807/983-2484 fax/message

Rossport Inn
Rossport, ON
P0T 2R0
807/824-3213

Superior Ecoventures
Site 3 Comp-23, RR13
Thunder Bay, ON
P7B 6B3
807/768-9499

Superior Fly Fishing
150 Egan Place
Thunder Bay, ON
P7A 2Y1
807/474-6501

Skinners
50 King St., East
Toronto, ON
M5C 1E5
416/863-9701

Karl Vogel
RR2
Goulais River, ON
P0S 1E0
705/649-3313

Wabusk Expeditions Ltd.
Xavier Chookomoolin
PO Box 255
Attawapiskat, ON
P0L 1A0
705/997-2282

Wilson's
26 Wellington St., East
Toronto, ON
M5E 1S2
416/869-3473

Winisk River Camps
Box 176
Webequie, ON
P0T 3A0
807/353-6531 (winter)
807/353-1595 (summer)

Appendix B
Fly Angler Travel Information

Ontario Ministry of Natural Resources Offices

Northwest Region
Atikokan
108 Saturn Avenue
Atikokan, Ontario
P0T 1C0
807/597 6971

Dryden
479 Government Road
Box 730
Dryden, Ontario
P8N 2Z4
807/223-3341

Fort Frances
922 Scott Street
Fort Frances, Ontario
P9A 1J4
807/274-5337

Geraldton
208 Beamish Avenue, W.
Box 640
Geraldton, Ontario
807/854-1030

Ignace
Box 448
Ignace, Ontario
P0T 1T0
807/934-2233

Kenora
808 Robertson Street
Box 5080
Kenora, Ontario
P9N 3X9
807/468-2501

Nipigon
Box 970
Nipigon, Ontario
P0T 2J0
807/887-5000

Red Lake
Box 5003
Red Lake, Ontario
P0V 2M0
807/727-2253

Sioux Lookout
Prince Street
Box 309
Sioux Lookout, Ontario
P0V 2T0
807/737-1140

Terrace Bay
Box 280
Terrace Bay, Ontario
P0T 2W0
807/825-3205

Thunder Bay
435 James St., S.
Suite B001
Thunder Bay, Ontario
P7E 6S8
807/475-1471

Northeast Region
Blind River
62 Queen St.
Box 190
Blind River, Ontario
P0R 1B0
705/356-2234

Chapleau
190 Cherry St.
Chapleau, Ontario
P0M 1K0
705/864-1710

Cochrane
2 Third Ave.
Box 730
Cochrane, Ontario
P0L 1C0
750/272-4365

Espanola
148 Fleming St.
Box 1340
Espanola, Ontario
P3E 1R8
705/869-1330

Gogama
2000 Low Avenue
Box 129
Gogama, Ontario
P0M 1W0
705/894-2000

Hearst
631 Front St.
Box 670
Hearst, Ontario
P0L 1N0
705/362-4346

Kapuskasing
RR2
Kapuskasing, Ontario
P5N 2X8
705/335-6191

Kirkland Lake
Box 129
Corner Hwy. 66 & 112
Kirkland Lake, Ontario
P0K 1T0
705/642-3222

Manitouwadge
Box 309
Manitouwadge, Ontario
P0T 2C0
807/826-3225

Moosonee
Box 190
Moosonee, Ontario
P0L 1Y0
705/336-2987

North Bay
3301 Trout Lake Road
North Bay, Ontario
P1A 4L7
705/475-5550

Sault Ste. Marie
60 Church Street
Sault Ste. Marie, Ontario
P6A 3H3
705/949-1231

Sudbury
3767 Hwy. 69 S.
Suite 5
Sudbury, Ontario
P3G 1E7
705/564-7823

Timmins
896 Riverside Drive
Timmins, Ontario
P4N 3W2
705/267-7951

Wawa
Box 1160
Wawa, Ontario
P0S 1K0
705/856-2396

Southcentral Region

Algonquin Park
P.O. Box 219
Whitney, Ontario
K0J 2M0
613/637-2780

Aurora, Greater Toronto
50 Bloomington Road W.
RR2
Aurora, Ontario
L4G 3G8
905/713-7400

Aylmer
353 Talbot St. W.
Aylmer, Ontario
N5H 2S8
519/773-9241

Bancroft
Box 500, Hwy. 28
Bancroft, Ontario
K0L 1C0
613/332-3940

Bracebridge
RR2, Hwy. 11 North
Bracebridge Ontario
P1L 1W9
705/645-8747

Chatham
1023 Richmond St., W.
Box 1168
Chatham, Ontariov
N7M 5L8
519/354-7340

Clinton
100 Don St.
Box 819
Clinton, Ontario
N0M 1L0
519/482-3428

Guelph
1 Stone Rd., W.
Guelph, Ontario
N1G 4Y2
519/658-9355

Kemptville
Postal Bag 2002
Concession Road
Kemptville, Ontario
K0G 1J0
613/258-8204

Kingston
Ontario Government Building
Beachgrove Complex
798 King St., N.
Kingston, Ontario
K7L 5S8
613/531-5700

Midhurst
Midhurst, Ontario
L0L 1X0
705/725-7500

Niagara
4890 Victoria Ave., N.
P.O. Box 5000
Vineland, Ontario
L0R 2E0
905/562-4147

Owen Sound
1450 Seventh Ave., E.
Owen Sound, Ontario
N4K 2Z1
519/376-3860

Parry Sound
7 Bay St.
Parry Sound, Ontario
P2A 1S4
705/746-4201

Pembroke
Riverside Dr.
Box 220
Pembroke, Ontario
K8A 6X4
613/732-3661

Peterborough
300 Water St.
P.O. Box 7000
Peterborough, Ontario
K9J 8M5
705/755-2001

Tweed
Postal Bag 70
Old Troy Road
Tweed, Ontario
K0K 3J0
613/478-2330

Ontario Tourism Agencies

Southwestern Ontario

Southwestern Ontario Travel Association
4023 Meadowbrook Drive,
Suite 112
London, Ontario
N6L 1E7
1-800-661-6804

Festival Country

Niagara and Mid-Western Ontario Travel Association
180 Greenwich Ave.
Brantford, Ontario
N3S 2X6
1-800-267-3399

Lakelands

Northern Ontario Tourist Outfitters (NOTO)
1-800-ONTARIO

Metropolitan Toronto

Tourism Toronto
807 Queen's Quay West,
Suite 509
P.O. Box 126
Toronto, Ontario
M51 1A7
1-800-363-1990

Getaway Country

Central Ontario Travel Association
P.O. Box 539
Bancroft, Ontario
K0L 1C0
1-800-461-1912

Ontario East

Almaguin Nipissing Travel Association
1040 Gardiners Road,
Suite B
Kingston, Ontario
K7P 1R7
1-800-387-0516

Rainbow Country

Rainbow Country Travel Association
2726 Whippoorwill Ave.
Sudbury, Ontario
P3G 1E9
1-800-465-6655

Algoma Country

Algoma Kinniwabi Travel Association
553 Queen St. East, Suite 1M
Sault Ste. Marie, Ontario
P6A 2A4
1-800-263-2546

James Bay Frontier

Cochrane Timiskaming Travel Association
76 McIntyre Road,
P.O. Box 920
Schumacher, Ontario
P0N 1G0
1-800-461-3766

North of Superior

North of Superior Tourism Association
1119 East Victoria Ave.
Thunder Bay, Ontario
P7C 1B7
1-800-265-3951

Sunset Country

Ontario's Sunset Country Travel Association
102 Main Street, Suite 201
P.O. Box 647M
Kenora, Ontario
P9N 3X6
1-800-665-7567

Other Agencies

Grand River Conservation Authority
400 Clyde Road
P.O. Box 729
Cambridge, ON
N1R 5W6
519/621-2761

Resorts Ontario
29 Albert St. North,
Orillia, Ontario
L3V 5J9
705/325-9115

Northern Ontario Native Tourism Association
Ste. 7 Comp-1554
RR4 Mission Road
Thunder Bay ON
P7C 4Z2
807/623-0497
www.tradenet.ca/NONTA

Northern Ontario Tourist Outfitters
(NOTO)
269 Main St., West
North Bay, Ontario
P1B 2T8
705/472-5552

Ontario North EcoTourism Network (ONE Network)
RR7, 4398 Hwy. 61
Thunder Bay, Ontario
P7C 5V5
807/964-2823

Treat yourself
and your angling partner . . .

...to a fly fishing and tying feast with subscriptions to *Flyfishing & Tying Journal*. You'll marvel at the helpful, colorful creativity inside this 100-plus-page quarterly masterpiece of publishing!

You've worked hard, now sit back and drink in the elixir of fly-fishing potential that we provide you, featuring fine printing on top-quality paper. We are terribly excited with our generous, friendly fly-fishing publication and know you will love it also! Please share our joy of discovery and subscribe today!

Strike a deal
for only $15.00 for one year.

Order a subscription below for you and your angling friend.

TO SUBSCRIBE
CALL
1-800-541-9498

(9-5 Monday thru Friday, Pacific Time)

Or Use The Coupon Below

- -

SUBSCRIBE/ORDER HERE!

Please send me:

☐ One year of *Flyfishing & Tying Journal* for only $15.00 (4 big issues)

☐ Two years of *Flyfishing & Tying Journal* for only $25.00 (8 issues)

☐ Check enclosed (US Funds)   ☐ New   ☐ Renew

☐ Charge to:

☐ Visa ☐ MC CC#:_____ Exp: _____

(Canadian & foreign orders please add $5/year)

Phone orders: 1-800-541-9498 or 503-653-8108. FAX 503-653-2766. Call 8 to 5 M-F, Pacific Standard Time.

Name: _____	Name: _____
Day Phone:(_____) _____	Day Phone:(_____) _____
Address: _____	Address: _____
_____	_____
City:_____ State:_____ Zip:_____	City:_____ State:_____ Zip:_____

FRANK AMATO PUBLICATIONS • P.O. BOX 82112 • PORTLAND, OR 97282